Time for a
STORY

Sharing Books with Infants and Toddlers

Time for a STORY

Sharing Books with Infants and Toddlers

Amy Brooks Read and

Saroj Nadkarni Ghoting

Gryphon House

www.gryphonhouse.com

Copyright

Published by Gryphon House, Inc.

P. O. Box 10, Lewisville, NC 27023

800.638.0928; 877.638.7576 (fax)

Visit us on the web at www.gryphonhouse.com.

Library of Congress Cataloging-in-Publication Data

The Cataloging-in-Publication Data is registered with the Library of Congress for ISBN: 978-0-87659-657-9

Bulk Purchase

Gryphon House books are available for special premiums and sales promotions as well as for fund-raising use. Special editions or book excerpts also can be created to specifications. For details, call 800-638-0928.

Disclaimer

Gryphon House, Inc., cannot be held responsible for damage, mishap, or injury incurred during the use of or because of activities in this book. Appropriate and reasonable caution and adult supervision of children involved in activities and corresponding to the age and capability of each child involved are recommended at all times. Do not leave children unattended at any time. Observe safety and caution at all times.

Table of Contents

Dedication

To Mike, Alden, and Hadyn,
Thanks for your patience. Yes, it's done! I love you all.

—A. B. R.

For all the dedicated early childhood educators who make a difference
in the lives of young children and their families every day.

—S. N. G.

Introduction

Preparing a child for school success begins at birth. Yes, even that early they begin building skills that will prepare them for kindergarten. When a child enters an early childhood classroom as an infant or young toddler, she is beginning her journey toward kindergarten. In those few short years, every experience matters. As early childhood providers, we have a responsibility to provide high-quality care and education. Ensuring that children's care is of the highest quality includes using early literacy (prereading) activities and experiences that support their growth and development, all day, every day.

Reading with infants and toddlers is a fundamental activity, which all children should experience. In child care, when you have a full class of infants and toddlers this can be demanding. Taking a book off the shelf and reading it is a fairly easy task. But, selecting the most appropriate book, reading it in a way that captures the children's attention, emphasizing in playful ways the skills and components that children need to develop, and incorporating the practices that help build early literacy skills can be challenging. It takes thought, preparation, and planning to make the most out of every experience a child has with a book. You may already be doing some of the techniques that we suggest, such as using voices for characters, making animal sounds, or singing songs. If so, great! We will offer more information about why each activity is developmentally appropriate and how it relates to building early literacy skills. This book has been developed to support early childhood professionals as well as parents and families with all the challenges of maximizing reading experiences with infants and toddlers to enhance their early literacy development.

The most important item or tool that a teacher or parent has in preparing children for later reading success is a book. With hundreds of thousands of children's books published each year, how do you select the right ones? What should the books include? How many words should they have? What kinds of pictures should they have? This book is not a critical review of children's books or an endorsement of any particular authors; it is a guide that covers different categories of books for infants and toddlers and explains how teachers and parents can use these books to help build the early literacy foundation that will take children from the infant and toddler years into preschool. Indeed, it is the way we use books with children that makes the difference in their early literacy development. The book is the tool, but it is you who makes a difference in children's language development in using that tool.

How This Book Is Organized

Chapter 1 explains how early literacy develops and how you can support young children as they develop the skills needed to learn to read. Chapters 2 through 6 focus on a particular type of book and how this type of book helps build on early literacy practices and components. The practices, components, and focus areas that are most closely tied to the type of book are included. The practice of "writing" is not specifically connected to any of the types of books but will be woven throughout all of the categories:

- Interactive Books
  - Practice—Play
  - Components—Background Knowledge, Print Awareness, Letter Knowledge
  - Focus—Sensory-Motor Development, Object Permanence, I Can Do It
- Song Books and Rhymes
  - Practice—Sing
  - Components—Phonological Awareness, Vocabulary
  - Focus—Rhythm and Rhyme, Action Rhymes
- Informational Books
  - Practice—Talk
  - Components—Background Knowledge, Vocabulary, Letter Knowledge
  - Focus—Learning about my World
- Stories
  - Practice—Read
  - Components—Background Knowledge, Print Awareness, Phonological Awareness, Vocabulary
  - Focus—Cognitive Development, Sequencing, Narrative Skills

Exposing children to a variety of types and styles of books not only helps build a strong early literacy foundation it helps build their excitement and interest in reading.

In the "What You Can Do with _____ Books" sections, we explore how a particular type of book addresses specific early literacy practices. We cover each practice—read, write, sing, talk, and play—and the skill or component that is addressed. Suggestions for ways to connect with parents and families or share information with them are included with each practice.

We have included books that are good examples of particular categories. They are only examples; the tips and suggestions can be used with just about any book. Be creative. Use books that you and the children like. As long as everyone is having fun, you will be able to enhance your story time with early literacy practices and components. In each chapter, we discuss how you can emphasize the characteristics of a particular type of book even if you do not have that specific title.

Each chapter includes sample book lists, which give a short summary or synopsis of the book and highlight features of the book. Following the book lists are examples of how to use selected titles.

Each chapter concludes with a sample story time for older toddlers and twos. Each sample includes the following information:

- Theme—for use if your curriculum is theme based
- Activity—what is happening
- Title—of a song, book, or rhyme
- Early Literacy Connection—explanation of what is happening or the reasoning for incorporating this in story time. This area includes information that can be shared with parents and families and often includes developmental information.
- Skill or Component—what area of early literacy is being targeted

Although specific titles are used for examples and sample story times, just about any book can be substituted. That way if the highlighted book is not available, you still have a stash of skills activities or techniques that can make the most of reading experiences. The information included addresses the early literacy development of children from infancy to age two. Some information addresses children who may be a little over twenty-four months since it is common for classes or family child-care homes to have mixed ages or not to move a child to another class when he is exactly twenty-four months.

The last two chapters in the book offer suggestions and tools that can be used to support early literacy in the classroom, connect with parents and families, and help teachers implement early literacy enhanced story times.

As you use this book, focus on what to do with the sample books and the early literacy connections that we highlight more than on the specific title itself. For example, we may use a book as an example and describe a particular technique for reading or an activity to use. Use those techniques and activities with other books as well. Just because you ask a particular question while reading a book about dogs does not mean you cannot ask a similar question while reading a book about trucks. Some of the suggestions may feel awkward at first; keep it up, and with practice they will become easier.

At first you may need to follow the suggestions step by step. As you become more comfortable with techniques, allow yourself to become more creative. Have fun while you are reading and talking with the children in your class. If you are having fun and enjoying literacy activities, they will also, and they will have more enjoyable experiences with books and reading. This puts children on the path to being ready for school!

Chapter 1

Getting Started

Babies come into the world ready to learn. Every day parents and early childhood teachers should be talking, singing, reading, writing, and playing with infants and toddlers. These activities not only help children develop in all areas—physical, cognitive, and social-emotional—but they also help build the foundation for later reading success. Children need all five of these practices to be ready for school and to be ready to learn how to read. At this age, birth to twenty-four months, we are not talking about teaching children how to read. The focus is on laying a strong foundation for later reading.

Early literacy is what children know about communication, language (verbal and nonverbal), reading, and writing before they can actually read or write. We must include and address early literacy components in our daily work with infants and toddlers. More detailed descriptions of the components and how they relate to infants and toddlers can be found in the table on page 113.

- **Phonological Awareness**—the ability to hear and play with the smaller sounds in words
- **Print Awareness**—knowing that print has meaning, understanding how to handle a book, understanding the direction of print, beginning to recognize the author and title, and noticing environmental print
- **Letter Knowledge**—knowing that the same letter can look different, understanding that letters have names and represent sounds, recognizing shapes, and understanding *alike* and *different*
- **Vocabulary**—knowing the meanings of words including names of objects, actions, feelings, concepts and ideas; learning the meaning of new words
- **Background Knowledge**—prior knowledge, what children already know, including print motivation and narrative skills

Let's look at each of the five practices—talking, singing, reading, writing, and playing—to see how they support early literacy.

Talking: Talking is the basis for all later literacy—early literacy and reading skills. Children need a strong basis in oral language and listening, speaking, and communication skills as a foundation for later literacy. The way we talk with children makes a big difference in their early literacy development. Talking with children from the time they are born, making eye contact, watching their gestures and responses, using words they are not familiar with as we are talking with them every day are all ways to support early literacy. It is important to talk with children a lot! In an early childhood classroom, there should be conversations happening all day.

Talking *to* children is not sufficient; we need to talk *with* them. Give them time to respond, even if they are not verbal yet. Pause for five to ten seconds after asking a question. This gives them time to formulate an answer or respond with cooing or babbling. Very young infants may respond by looking at you, kicking their feet, or moving their hands.

Children need to hear a lot of words while they are young; this helps them build a strong, large vocabulary. Vocabulary and oral language are strongly connected to reading comprehension. Building vocabulary begins in infancy. Research has shown that a gap in vocabulary development can be seen as early as six months and is strongly apparent by eighteen months. Talking about things that are not present, that happened, or that will happen; explaining what we are doing; asking questions that must be answered with more than yes or no; and encouraging babies to babble and toddlers to talk are small but important ways to support language development. Children who enter school with a large vocabulary, having heard many words and words repeated many times, will have an easier time understanding what they read. They will also find it easier to sound out words they have heard before.

Singing: Singing slows down language. It takes us longer to sing a rhyme than it does to say it. Children can hear the sounds of language more easily when we sing. Also, there is a distinct note for each syllable, so children hear words broken down into parts, which will help them later sound out words when they learn to read. Songs often have interesting words that we do not hear in regular conversation.

Reading: Reading aloud to children is the single most important activity to help children become successful readers. However, the *way* we read with children makes a difference. Reading the words in the book is important because sometimes books use interesting words we do not use in regular conversation with young children. It is also important to talk about what is

---

CHILDREN AND SCREEN TIME

Parents may ask you about television and using technology and apps with very young children. Here are a few points to share with them:

When a very young child is riveted to the screen, we might assume it is because she is interested. However, young children are particularly sensitive to the *orienting reflex*, which makes the brain automatically focus attention on new sights or sounds.

Studies have shown that passive screen time can take away from time that adults play with their children, which is when children learn how to interact with others and learn language.

happening in the pictures of the book and to help children relate what is happening to their own experiences. This helps later with comprehension. By occasionally pointing to the pictures and words in the book, we help children develop print awareness, understand how books work, and understand that print has meaning.

Helping children enjoy books goes a long way when they are later being taught to read in school. Books are a great way for children to learn about the world around them, about other people, places, and things. Children who have had enjoyable experiences around books and reading are more likely to stick with learning to read even if it is difficult for them.

Writing: Writing may seem like an activity for older children, but writing skills start early. Even babies like to grasp your finger! Later, they will use the pincer grasp by picking up small items with their index finger and thumb. The small motor skills you do with them, from clapping to fingerplays, will help develop the finger and hand movements needed for writing. Scribbling is the beginning of writing, so encourage them to write, and make sure they see you writing, too.

Playing: There are so many ways to play. Children learn best through play and exploration. Putting words to their play—narrating and commenting on what they are doing, what they feel when they touch something, and the characteristics of items—are all ways to bring language to what they observe in their world. You can tell stories using props, follow their lead as they play, and play simple games such as peekaboo.

As they get older, they will start to have one item represent another. They will play with objects such as dolls or blocks; for example, a block may be used as a truck. This kind of symbolic thinking is also used in language development when they realize that the picture of the truck or the word *truck* is not the real truck but represents, or is a symbol for, the real truck.

Talking, singing, reading, writing, and playing, and the early literacy components—phonological awareness, print awareness, letter knowledge, vocabulary, and background knowledge—support each other. How we do the practices with the children makes a difference in whether or not we are supporting their early literacy development. In the following section we give some examples of how each of the practices can support the early literacy components. You can also see how the early literacy components can be put into practice in so many ways, as we talk, sing, read, write, and play with children throughout the day.

Talking

Phonological Awareness: Babies learn the sounds of the languages they hear. When we speak with them in *parentese*—using normal adult language but saying the words at a higher pitch, drawing out the vowels, speaking very clearly, and repeating words—we help them learn language. Until they are about nine months old, babies are better able to hear the sounds of language and will listen longer when we speak in parentese.

Talk about environmental sounds, such as the doorbell ringing, a cell phone beeping, a honking car, birds singing, a dog barking, and so on. Make animal sounds as a start to help babies focus on sounds. Say nursery rhymes to help children hear the lilt of language as well as rhyming words. Especially as they move into toddlerhood, specifically point out the rhyming words in nursery rhymes. Help young children notice beginning sounds of words by pointing out words that begin with the same sound, such as *disposable diaper*. Have fun playing with words and sounds.

Print Awareness: The first step of helping children understand that print has meaning is to point out and read signs, logos, and labels. For toddlers, you might hold a favorite book upside-down or start reading it backward from the last page. Encourage children to talk about what is "wrong" with the way you are reading the book. When a book shows a picture of an item, show the real item. For example, if you have a ball available and a book shows a picture of a ball and the word *ball*, take time to show the child the picture of the ball and then also the real ball. This will help the child make the connection that the picture and the text represent a real thing.

Letter Knowledge: Letter knowledge is more than just recognizing letters. Because children recognize letters by their shapes, we have lots of opportunities to talk about and to help them feel shapes. Talk about the characteristics, such as texture and color, of the items they see and touch. Talking about the characteristics of objects helps young children focus on these characteristics and, later, to compare objects—what is similar and what is different. For toddlers, you can help them make the comparisons: Which one is bigger? taller? longer? This helps them later to distinguish between similar letters. A great place to start is with the letters in the child's name. Talk about the shapes in the letters.

Vocabulary: Helping children know the meanings of words starts young, just by hearing lots of words. Because children learn vocabulary best through situations, talking as we are doing things together helps them understand words through context and gestures. Speaking in parentese helps young children have a larger vocabulary because they listen to you longer. Be sure to add new words to baby's babble and to toddler's talking, using synonyms or further description. And don't be afraid to use "big words." Children will never know them if you don't use them.

It is important not only to talk about objects but also about feelings—giving words to how they and you might be feeling throughout the day during specific situations. Use words for ideas as well, such as *cooperation* and *responsibility*. Even if children do not know the exact meanings of these words, they will learn them as you use them repeatedly.

Background Knowledge: Because background knowledge covers such a wide area, there are so many ways to support it. You are supporting background knowledge when you compare and contrast objects. Putting processes in sequence, such as first putting on a sock and then putting on a shoe, helps children's conceptual thinking. Be sure to support children's problem-solving abilities. Don't be too quick to fix things for them. If they are really stumped on what to do in a situation, offer a clue instead of the answer. You can also explain how you are thinking when you are deciding what to do or how to do something. When they hear you explaining your thinking, you are modeling problem-solving skills.

Children love to learn about the world, so tell them what you know on a variety of topics, and encourage them to tell you what they know. You may or may not understand all they say, but your encouraging attitude helps to develop their language. It often takes five to twelve seconds for toddlers to respond to what you say, so give them the extra time they need. As they become more used to using language, they will need less time to respond.

Have conversations about everyday routines such as diapering and snack time. Talk not only about what is happening now but also about things that happened in the past and things that are going to happen in the future. As children get close to two years old, they may begin to be able to tell a little story or tell you what happened.

Singing

Phonological Awareness: Sing with children, even if you feel you cannot carry a tune. Singing helps children hear smaller sounds in words because words are drawn out. They hear each syllable because there is a distinct note for each syllable. Sing songs with animal sounds or with silly and nonsense words!

Print Awareness: When you use song books, point out words in the chorus or repeated lines. Try singing, "Oh, no! My book is upside down!" to the tune of "London Bridge Is Falling Down." You can use song cards or print the words to songs on large paper, occasionally pointing to the words you are singing.

Letter Knowledge: If you choose to sing the alphabet song, which is usually sung to the tune of "Twinkle, Twinkle, Little Star," try singing it to the tune of "Mary Had a Little Lamb" instead. This encourages more emphasis on saying the letters and avoids the common run-together pronunciation or mumbling of *L, M, N, O*. Other songs such as "BINGO" use the names of the letters. You can also sing songs that talk about shapes.

Vocabulary: Some songs and rhymes have words not heard in everyday conversation with young children, such as *fetch* in the rhyme "Jack and Jill." Many songs help children with concepts such as opposites, sizes, and shapes. For example, "Pease Porridge Hot" and "The Noble Duke of York" feature opposites: hot and cold and up and down.

Background Knowledge: Knowing common rhymes and songs helps support children's background knowledge; it is cultural knowledge. When we use songs that go through a sequence, such as "This is the way we . . .," or songs with a story, such as "Mary Had Little Lamb," we support children's conceptual thinking. Many songs help children with concepts such as numbers and size.

Reading

Phonological Awareness: As you share books with young children, there are many ways to support phonological awareness, or hearing the smaller sounds in words. This awareness will later help them sound out words when they learn to read. Many books for babies and toddlers have animals in them. Whether or not the sounds that the animals make are actually written out in the text, you can make the sounds and have the children try to repeat the sounds. When you read nursery rhyme books, children are hearing the lilt of language and hearing rhyming words. Reading books that incorporate songs helps support phonological awareness. Books that have *alliteration*, or a repeated beginning sound, such as *Busy Birdies* by John Schindel, expose children to hearing that individual sound. When you share a book with rhyming words, tell the children which words rhyme. Repeat reading the book often—some toddlers and young twos may chime in with the rhyming word if you pause right before reading it.

Print Awareness: Knowing that print has meaning and how to handle books develops from encouraging babies to explore books and to notice the world around them. Babies explore objects with their mouths; they will chew on a book. They are getting to know what books are like. They do not have a lot of coordination with their hands and may bat at or hit the book. They may try to imitate your turning the pages of the book even though they are not yet coordinated enough to really turn the pages. This is a beginning. Be sure to have some board books around that you know will be chewed on and beaten up. At this stage, it's okay.

As you look at a book with a young child, point to the words in the title and to some of the words in the book, perhaps a repeated phrase. This is how children come to understand that it is the text we are reading, not the pictures.

Letter Knowledge: Because children learn to identify letters by their shapes, pointing out shapes in shape books is a good first step. We can see shapes all around us, but there are many books with clear and colorful pictures of the shapes. Because so many letters look quite similar, children try to notice how they look different. Of course, some differences don't matter: An *N* is an *N* no matter what color it is, but it turns into a *Z* when you turn it on its side. The difference between an *n* and an *h* is the height of the line. So, by helping children notice how objects look similar or different—even when we are not talking about letters—we help pave the way to later letter knowledge.

Vocabulary: Some books, even simple books such as *Dear Zoo* by Rod Campbell, use interesting words like *fierce*, *fragile*, and *danger*. These are words that we may not use in regular conversation with young children. Using informational or factual books with children offers them different words than the ones we find in stories, so be sure to use these books as well.

Sometimes books for young children have only one or two words on a page. Then, we depend upon you to have conversations around the book to add more language that builds their vocabulary.

Background Knowledge: Children learn so much about the world through observing, exploring, and hearing you talk about the things around them. Books offer opportunities to expose children to things they may not be able to see in their own environments. Books are a window to the world. Choose books on topics that the child shows interest in; offer several books and allow the child to choose. This will help the child develop an enjoyable relationship with books. As you read the book together, give the child some time to talk about the pictures in the book. This will help you to understand what the child might be thinking or where his attention is directed. Be sure to relate what is happening in the book to the child's experiences, even if the child cannot understand everything you say. This approach helps later to develop comprehension.

We want children to relate enjoyment to books and reading, so having them join in and participate as you share books together will keep them more happily engaged. When you are reading a book you really enjoy, tell the child how much you like it and what you like about it. Reading with expression is one way to keep their attention. You can use props, flannel or magnet boards, or puppets as you tell and retell stories. If the child loses interest, you can try at another time.

Writing

Phonological Awareness: You might try drawing a picture of an animal or an item that makes a sound and then talk about the sound it makes. Draw a picture and say a rhyming word or a word that starts with the same sound.

Print Awareness: You can make a simple book out of folded paper and have children write or draw in their own books. If you like, you can write down what they tell you is happening in their drawings. Make age-appropriate writing materials available, and encourage scribbling and drawing.

Letter Knowledge: Encouraging children to draw shapes and make lines and drawings are first steps to later being able to write letters. You can encourage children to write with their fingers in the air, too.

Vocabulary: Encourage children to draw pictures and tell you about them. Add a new word or two to what the children are saying, or clarify meanings of words they are using. Describe children's scribbles: "You drew a big blue line."

Background Knowledge: Have children draw pictures for a story. Ask them to tell you what the pictures are and write what they say. This will help them learn how stories work. Let children see you write, and explain what you are writing. This will begin to teach them that there are different purposes for writing. Sing and recite fingerplays and action rhymes. Learning the movements helps to develop the fine motor skills needed for using writing utensils.

Playing

Phonological Awareness: Help children become aware of sounds as they play. Clap out words into syllables. Point out sounds that some of their toys make. Books are often a baby's first toy. Keep books with animal sounds and rhymes where babies and children can easily play with and explore them.

Print Awareness: Make books that include pictures of the children in the classroom engaging in play. Add print to play by including signs and labels for familiar objects. Use signs with blocks, label storage containers with words and pictures for manipulatives and toys, and make books available in all play areas.

Letter Knowledge: Play with puzzles and blocks—with so many shapes, colors, sizes, there are lots of ways to sort and categorize. Play matching and sorting games; notice what is alike and different and include foam, magnet, and block letters. Don't worry about having the children identify the letters. Just let them feel and play with them.

Vocabulary: As babies handle objects and toys, describe how the toys feel, what they look like, and the sounds they make. Enhance children's play by adding new words and descriptions to the words or babbles they use as they play. Children learn new words best when they learn them in context, so playing is a great time to introduce new words. Playtime allows for pretending. You can put words to feelings—the characters they are playing, the children's feelings, and your own feelings.

Background Knowledge: Play is a good way to develop background knowledge through role playing different situations, such as a restaurant, doctor's office, school, car repair shop, or library. Dramatic play and acting out stories together helps children get a sense of story structure. You can use puppets or props. Provide toys that can represent the characters in a favorite book to act out the book or extend the story in imaginative play.

Story Times for Infants and Toddlers

> **TIP**
>
> Remember, even when you are conducting a scheduled story time or circle time, young children should always have the choice of participating.

So, you understand the value of reading with infants and toddlers, but how can you do it effectively? Reading with very young children should be flexible. As one teacher in an infant room said, "You just have to go with the flow." Remember, even when you are conducting a scheduled story time or circle time, young children should always have the choice of participating.

Flexibility is important, but it is essential to have purpose, intention, and structure when you are reading. If not, there will be many missed opportunities. Even very young infants should be read to throughout every day. Reading times can range from informal activities to more structured activities. Children can quickly learn and be able to predict what happens next if there is a structure or schedule to their daily reading time. Begin your story time with a particular song, rhyme, or chant—they will know when they hear it that it is time for books!

Getting through a certain number of books does not ensure an effective story time. Sometimes just one book is enough if you include additional activities and incorporate techniques that help build children's skills. Adjust the length, number of books, songs, rhymes, and activities to your particular group. You know the children in your class best; design the story time to fit their needs and abilities. As you are reading, observe the children. Watch for cues and behaviors that let you know if they are paying attention, interested, bored, tired, and so on. This will help as you plan which books to include in a story time.

This is a sample format that would be appropriate for toddlers. Story times with infants will be much shorter and less formal than those with older babies. Lap reading should happen throughout the day with the children. We have provided a reproducible template in Appendix A to assist with planning story-time activities.

- **Opening song or rhyme:** Use the same one each time. There are a variety of examples throughout this book, or you can make up your own, search online for songs, or use shakers or bells to signify the start of story time. If you choose to use shakers, bells, or other sounds, make sure to explain the meaning of the sound to the children.
- **Introduction:** Tell the children what is happening. "It's time to read books!" or "Today we are going to read about _____."
- **Two to four songs or rhymes:** Adjust the number for your age group. Repeat them a couple of times so the children begin to learn them. You can also repeat songs and rhymes from previous story times. Clap once between each song to indicate that it is over. Depending on your group's abilities and interest, mix up action rhymes with quieter ones. Add puppets or story gloves to maintain interest.
- **Read one book.**

- **Two to four songs or rhymes:** Again, adjust the number to meet the needs of your group. Use this time to get your next book ready. Avoiding waiting time can save your story time.
- **Read one book.** This is a good time to switch to a different type of book, either a different format, such as a big book, a lap-size board book, or a hardcover book. Or, choose a book from a different category, such as a storybook, an informational book, a book to sing, and so on.
- **Use a flannel story, puppet, or story glove:** These can be used to tell a story, sing a song, or reinforce topics and concepts. You can use additional props such as music, blocks, items that are represented in the books you have read, scarves, or musical instruments.
- **Closing song or rhyme:** Use the same one each time.

Planning story times for infants and toddlers can be challenging. They are typically quite a bit shorter than story times for older two-year-olds and preschoolers. With newly mobile children who are practicing their toddling skills, sitting to listen to book after book is not going to happen on most days. Although the story times are shorter in length, that does not mean that you will spend less time planning and preparing. Keep the following in mind when you are planning your story times:

- Use books that you like to read. Repetition is good. Reread books that you and the children like.
- Determine what your purpose is—Why this particular book or song? What do you want to accomplish? Remember, having fun and enjoying books is often a very good goal!
- Practice, read the book through, and plan what you would like to do with it—sing it, add props, tell a story about it, retell it after reading.
- Gather all of the items you will need and have them ready before story time begins.
- Plan, write down vocabulary you want to introduce, questions you want to ask, the words to new songs you are going to sing, along with any special notes or reminders.
- Get more information on any topic you are going to cover that you may need additional information on—use the Internet, access resource books, contact your local library, or ask coworkers and colleagues.
- Reflect—After implementing a planned story time or literacy activity, review what worked and what could be improved. Were the children interested? Why or why not?
- Challenge yourself—Ask a coteacher or other staff person to observe your story time and give you feedback. (We provide a sample observation tool in Chapter 6.)

Reading with Infants

Ideally, reading with infants should be done one-on-one with the child in your lap looking at the book with you. This is definitely easier to accomplish for parents and families, at home or in a library story-time setting. When you have a class full of infants, it can be more challenging to read with each child individually. You can only fit so many children on your lap! Try laying a book on the floor and facing the baby while you are reading. The text will be upside down for you, but you can watch to see where baby is looking. This will give you opportunities to follow the baby's lead and interest.

Pick times of day when children are rested, and choose books about things that children are familiar with. Allow the infants to pat and chew on the books—remember, they are learning through all of their senses. Repeat simple books, songs, and rhymes, and read in a high-pitched voice to get the child's attention. Say the words slowly and clearly. As you read, look at and talk about the pictures, and point out words in the book. Allow children time to respond to the reading or pictures or to imitate you, even if they are not verbal yet.

Reading with Toddlers

Once they are mobile, getting children to sit and listen offers its challenges. Participation should always be voluntary. That being said, if you read it, they will come. When children hear the opening song that they associate with reading books, they will most likely move to the area designated for reading. If not, that's okay. Start reading, and you will soon have an audience.

Show enthusiasm and excitement about reading—your excitement is contagious! Repeat favorite books, stories, and songs, and allow the children to pick books for you to read. Use your voice; make animal sounds; change your pitch; give characters different voices; incorporate a lot of repetitive sounds, words, rhymes, and gestures; and vary your speed and volume as you read. Give the children time to repeat words or short phrases, and encourage them to make sounds when looking at the pictures. Allow the children to turn pages. Choose books about things the children are interested in and about familiar objects and subjects, such as family, food, and toys. Make a variety of books available. Tell stories to the children, and encourage them to tell stories to you.

Chapter 2

Interactive Books

What's the Connection?

- Practice: Play
- Components:
  - Background Knowledge
  - Print Awareness
  - Focus
  - Sensory Development
  - Object Permanence

Any book can be interactive with infants and toddlers—all they need is you. When you are reading with very young children, the more interactive the experience the better. Reading interactively simply means that there is interaction between you and the children. Interactive reading is not you reading to the children, and the children just sitting and quietly listening to the story. There should be a lot of talking, laughing, playing, and even singing. The more you engage them, the more fun and exciting the story time is for all of you. There are books designed specifically to engage the youngest readers and spark their interest and natural curiosity. In fact, research has shown that interactive reading supports children's early literacy skills.

Make sure to plan and use interactive books, songs, and fingerplays every day. They help build all of the skills that very young children need to develop to be ready for reading. Interactive books can be used one-on-one or in small groups. They are appropriate for both infants and toddlers. An additional benefit of interactive books is that, because of their unique design, they also support sensory development.

What to Look For

- Texture
- Lift-the-flap
- Moving parts
- Pull tabs
- Die-cut pages

Books for the youngest children typically have few words on each page. Using interactive books gives you something else you can do when you are reading together. Because they are learning through all of their senses, young children want to touch, smell, taste, hear, and see it all. Interactive books give you the opportunity to do just about all of that while reading. Most interactive books, particularly ones with flaps, tabs, and holes, have some things in common. For example, with these books you can easily use positional words with children because of the way they are made. There are pictures behind, under, beside, and so on. These types of books, which often include that peekaboo aspect, are developmentally appropriate for this age because young children are learning about object permanence. They are learning that, even if you do not see something, it still exists.

What You Can Do with Interactive Books

Interactive books are a great way to help build skills that infants and toddlers need and to encourage their love of books, reading, and stories. Books that offer the opportunity for the child to do something help them build mastery of tasks and the sense of "I can do it!"

These types of books, along with books that can be imitated or mimicked, are most closely tied to the practice of play. Play is fun! It is also how children learn about themselves, relationships, and the world around them. True play has the following aspects for the child:

- Enjoyment and pleasure around the activity
- Active engagement—the child is involved and shows interest
- Internal motivation—the child wants to do it
- Freedom from external rules—the rules are agreed upon and understood by the children
- Process rather than product—the value is in the doing not the result
- Can involve pretend or fantasy as children get older, such as a make-believe world to experiment with limits, roles, and power

There is purpose to play, and it is an essential practice in building a foundation for being ready to learn to read. For play to really be *play*, the child should initiate it. Follow the child's lead. With infants and toddlers who may not be very mobile or verbal, we have to pay attention to their reactions and engagement. At any sign of distress or frustration, move to another activity. Interactive books incorporate all of the practices that support children's growth and development.

Play

TIP

Imitating and mimicking your behaviors, gestures, and actions is the beginning of pretend play for babies. Give them lots of praise and encouragement when you see them imitate something you have done.

Infants and toddlers treat books like they are toys—they play with them. They like to put them in their mouths, pull them, push them, and tear them. Let young children explore and play as they learn how to handle books and build their background knowledge, and use positive redirection if they are getting too rough. Over time, you can teach them how to turn pages and take care of books instead of intentionally destroying them. Giving them time to explore and play with books is how children learn these important pieces of getting ready to learn how to read.

Interactive books help teach young ones that things and people exist even when you do not see them. Developmentally, this is referred to as *object permanence*, and it begins to develop between four and seven months. As you read and play with books that have flaps and tabs, encourage children to look for what is hidden. Reinforce their actions with excitement. Each time you exclaim, "There it is!" you are helping children learn object permanence. By about eight months, babies typically have a stronger grasp of this concept. Once they understand that the picture will be under the flap, you can move on to guessing games. Encourage children to make predictions about what might be under the flap or behind the tab. Keep this fun and positive—incorrect answers are learning opportunities. Play guessing games about what is behind a flap or through a peep hole. Many times, enough of the picture shows to give children clues to the picture that comes next. Learning how to predict what is going to happen helps children begin to build on their ability to narrate. This is a helpful skill as they begin to learn to read and learn about story structure. The development of object permanence and the ability to guess or predict what is unseen are all part of the background knowledge that children need to develop to be ready to learn to read.

Lifting flaps and pulling tabs can be considered *practice play*, which is play that involves repetition of actions and movements. Because interactive books typically have flaps, tabs, or holes on almost every page, children have the opportunity to repeat the action over and over.

Aside from using books designed for play, you can play with books that foster engagement in activities such as imitating the movements in the book or mimicking what is happening in the illustrations and pictures. Children have to learn how to imitate before they can move into pretend play. It is common for books designed for infants and toddlers to focus on what babies do, what kinds of activities they like, and movements they are capable of. When you read books that show children jumping, clapping, dancing, crawling, or wiggling, play along! Encourage the children to imitate the actions. Young children look to us to guide them, and when we are playing with a book, having fun and imitating the actions, it tells them that this is okay. Books can be a useful tool in supporting imitative play, and these activities not only support background knowledge, they also help develop print motivation. Children begin to learn that reading is fun!

Incorporate literacy activities into your daily curriculum to foster play and early literacy development. Imitate the actions that are in books. Bouncing, wiggling, and waving actions are fun for babies to do. When they hear you name the actions while reading the book and then again while you are playing and adding actions, you help children build their vocabulary and background knowledge. Make your own sensory (texture) books or texture boards for the children to play with during the day. Describe the textures as children feel them, talk about the similarities and differences. Again, these types of activities are directly tied to vocabulary and background knowledge development.

Keep books accessible that are made of durable materials and have rounded corners; stay away from sharp edges for the youngest children. Know and expect that some books will be loved a lot. They will begin to show wear and tear. To avoid frustration or disappointment when a class favorite becomes too torn up, make sure to designate some books for exploration and some for teacher use. Allowing children the freedom to explore and play with books helps them learn how books work, which helps them develop print awareness. They will be more comfortable handling books and will enjoy reading more.

Family Connection

Encourage parents and families to keep books available at all times. They can store them in baskets, crates, or on low shelves so the children can reach them. For nonmobile children, remind parents to offer books often and regularly. As children become mobile, they can initiate reading and playing with books on their own. Remind parents that it is okay for children to play with and even chew on books. There should always be a couple of books that they know are going to get damaged and then others that they share one-on-one with young children so the books do not so easily get damaged.

Read

Babies begin communicating with gestures. Pay attention to a baby's cues and gestures while you are reading with him. He may bat at a page, kick his legs, or pull the book to his mouth. These are indications that the baby is engaged in the reading activity. Have fun with these books. Young children are just beginning to build relationships with books and reading. If you are having fun, they will too.

- Laugh
- Give characters different voices
- Make positive statements, such as, "I love this book," "This is a funny story," and "The pictures are so pretty."
- Change the inflection of your voice—avoid reading in a monotone voice
- Make the books come alive by adding different voices and movements
- Get excited about what is under a flap or behind a tab
- Talk about the textures in a touch-and-feel book

Children who enjoy and are comfortable with books are more likely to stick with learning how to read later on.

In the classroom, keep children engaged with books and reading. This can be challenging, as within any individual class there are different developmental levels as well as individual interests. Interactive books are a good addition to your class library and reading times because, by design, they engage children. Just remember that the interaction really comes from us.

Here are a few points to keep in mind to maintain the children's interest and engagement while you read. If the story is getting too long or they are losing interest, change the sound of your voice or move the flaps and tabs to keep them engaged. It is okay if you do not read every word on the page—keep the experience fun and positive. Young toddlers may treat pictures like they are real objects; they may, for example, pet a picture that has fur. Make comments and describe what they are doing, and encourage these types of behaviors. Finally, rotate, change, or add books to the classroom to maintain interest. Repeated readings of books are very beneficial and a necessary activity for early literacy development, so keep the favorites on the shelf. However, adding new books will keep children interested in the book area of the classroom. Engaging children in fun reading activities and maintaining a high level of interaction help build their enjoyment of books and reading.

Set up a small display in your classroom to show parents a variety of interactive books. Hang a poster that highlights the benefits of books that encourage interaction, imitation, and mimicking.

Write

As young children learn to handle books, they are not only beginning a foundation of prereading skills, but they are also developing prewriting skills. Very young children will touch textures in books with their whole hands. As they develop more physical control, they will be able to touch with just a finger, which helps them prepare for writing as they enjoy the book. Pulling tabs, lifting flaps, and turning pages help develop the eye-hand coordination and dexterity needed for writing. These motor activities are important factors of print awareness.

When they are older, children will begin to understand that print has meaning and that there is a relationship between what is being read or sung and the printed text. We can help young children develop print awareness by writing the words to songs and rhymes on large cards. Allow children to point to, hold, and touch the cards. You can also occasionally point to words as you read or sing them. Play peekaboo with the cards: cover them with a blanket or cloth, and ask, "Where did the words go?" Pause for their response or to let them move the cloth. When the words are revealed, say, "There they are!"

Family Connection

Explain that reading and writing develop together, and it is as important to let children see their family members writing as it is to see them reading. Encourage parents and families to interact with their child during writing activities:

- Hold your infant facing the paper as you write checks for bills.
- Let your child sit on your lap as you make a grocery list.
- Let your toddler hold the list at the store and even help mark off items.
- Encourage your child to scribble—this is the beginning of writing.
- Allow your child to turn the pages and lift the flaps in books to help develop eye-hand coordination and to learn how books work.

Sing

There are some books written specifically for singing, but you can sing just about any book for infants and toddlers. The text is short, so you can add a little rhythm to your voice and make it a song. This will grab their attention because it sounds different from regular reading. Singing songs with babies and toddlers helps them hear words being broken up into smaller sounds. Each syllable has its own note. For children to be able to sound out words later when they are learning to read, they need to be comfortable playing with the parts of words and to be able to hear the smaller sounds, such as beginning and ending sounds. When we sing with children we are helping build these skills, which are part of phonological awareness.

We can reinforce ideas, themes, and concepts by pairing a related song or rhyme with a book. For example, after reading *Where Is Baby's Belly Button?* by Karen Katz, sing "Head, Shoulders, Knees, and Toes" and touch the parts of the body. Singing is fun for even the youngest baby. We can use singing not only to soothe and calm a child but as a teaching tool also. Every time we reinforce a concept for a child, we are helping her build the background knowledge needed to later read and understand information.

Family Connection

Make sure to give parents and families the actions as well as the words to songs. They will be able to reinforce children's learning of the gestures by singing and acting out the song at home. Remind parents and families that they do not have to be a able to carry a tune. Children don't care if you do it perfectly—they just like to sing!

Talk

When you share interactive books with children, the way you talk with them can help build their vocabulary as well as their background knowledge. Children need to develop a large vocabulary to be ready to learn how to read when they are older, and vocabulary learning begins as early as infancy. When you are reading an interactive book, add information about what you see in the picture or about something you know that is related to the pictures. Exposing children to information and language later helps them understand what they read. Use positional words, such as *under*, *inside*, *beside*, and *behind*. Children will begin to learn their meanings as you lift, pull, and move parts of the book.

Even if the children in your class are not verbal yet or have limited language, encourage them to talk about the pictures in the book, guess what is under the flap, or say what they see through the die-cut page. You might not understand everything they are saying or babbling, but you are giving them a chance to talk about the book—the language will come. Add to the fun by asking questions such as, "Where is . . . ," "Who is . . . ," and "What is . . . ." Always pause for about five to ten seconds, even if the child is too young to answer. Then answer the question yourself. This begins to teach that conversation has a give-and-take, speak-and-listen pattern. Raise your voice at the end of the question; this gives the cue that a response is expected. Children learn very quickly that, when your voice rises when asking a question, a response is expected.

Family Connection

Make a list of prepositional words that you have introduced to the children. Hang it on the door, wall, or bulletin board. Point it out to parents, and explain that children begin to learn the meaning of these words very quickly. They can use them throughout the day with their child and when they are reading books!

PREPOSITIONS

About	During	Over
Above	Except	Past
Across	Following	Plus
After	For	Regarding
Against	From	Since
Ahead of	In	Than
Along	In addition to	Through
Among	Including	To
Around	Inside	Toward
As	Instead of	Under
At	Into	Underneath
Before	Like	Unlike
Behind	Near	Until
Below	Next to	Up
Beneath	Off	Upon
Beside	On	With
Between	Onto	Within
Beyond	Opposite	Without
By	Out	
Down	Outside	

Lift-the-Flap and Die-Cut Books

These types of books support the development of object permanence (knowing that something is still there even if you cannot see it). By lifting flaps or looking through holes, children see items that, at first glance, are not there.

Bauer, Marion Dane. 2003. *Toes, Ears, and Nose!* New York: Little Simon.

> The bright colors and diverse faces will definitely catch a little one's attention. The rhyming guessing game of finding out what is under pieces of clothing help children learn body parts as well as practice their predicting skills.

Campbell, Rod. 2007. *Dear Zoo.* New York: Little Simon.

> This book may have been around for a while but it is still a popular pick for little ones. The flaps and text reveal enough to keep children guessing which animal the zoo sent. The story includes descriptive words that help build young children's vocabulary, such as *fierce, scary,* and *grumpy.* Remember to explain words that children may not know yet.

Christian, Cheryl. 2004. *Where's the Baby?/¿Dónde Está el Bebé?* Cambridge, MA: Star Bright.

> Christian's series includes a photo-flap board books and peekaboo books, and many of the titles are bilingual in a variety of languages. The books include real photographs of children and a simple text that keeps children guessing.

Cimarusti, Maria Torres. 1998. *Peek-a-Moo!* New York: Dutton Juvenile.

> This sturdy-page book (not a board book) includes large flaps for children to lift. Each reveals a familiar animal and the sound that it makes. The text naturally lends itself to a peekaboo guessing game.

DK Publishing. 2010. *Baby Pets!* New York: Dorling Kindersley.

> This title is part of the Baby Chunky Board Books series from DK Publishing. Other titles include *Baby: Night Night!, Baby: Colors!, Baby: Baa Baa!,* and *Baby: Hide and Seek!* In *Baby Pets!* the colorful pages are paired with photographs of cute pets. Descriptive words are used throughout: *stripy, shiny,* and *bright* are just a few.

Gershator, Phillis. 2010. *Who's in the Forest?* Concord, MA: Barefoot.

> The rhyming, rhythmic text of this book is easy to read and even set to a little tune if you want to sing it. Each die-cut hole gives a clue to which animal is next. With older children, encourage them to participate in the repeated phrase, "Who's in the forest, dark and deep?"

Hill, Eric. 2003. *Where's Spot?* New York: Putnam Juvenile.

> Spot is a tried-and-true favorite for many children. They quickly learn which animals are hiding where, and this gives a strong sense of accomplishment for young ones. Remember to add animal sounds to make this a very fun read.

Horacek, Petr. 2001. *Strawberries Are Red.* Somerville, MA: Candlewick Press.

> The die cut is the final surprise in this book. The shaped pages build to a finale that shows a fruit salad. This simple, colorful book builds on fruit names and colors.

Katz, Karen. 2000. *Where Is Baby's Belly Button?* New York: Little Simon.

This lift-the-flap book is made with large flaps that are easy for little fingers to begin moving. The cute babies in this book play peekaboo with body parts. The flaps introduce the positional words *under* and *behind*.

Laden, Nina. 2000. *Peek-a Who?* San Francisco, CA: Chronicle.

Laden also has a similar title, *Peek-a Zoo!*, which is just as fun to read and play with. These books have a simple rhyming text that keeps children guessing what comes next. The colorful pictures have a lot of contrast that helps keep babies' attention and focus. And, always a hit with young ones, there is a mirror in the back for peek-a-you!

Ziefert, Harriett. 2009. *Furry Friends: Same and Different.* Maplewood, NJ: Blue Apple.

This title is part of the Flip-a-Face series. Other titles include *Who Is Sleeping? Who Is Awake?*, *Baby Animals*, *Big Little*, *Colors*, and *Woof-Woof*. Cut outs in *Furry Friends* change a plain face into animal faces. The questions posed in the book about same and different may be difficult for toddlers; however, you can explain and describe the similarities and differences.

How to Read It: *Where Is Baby's Belly Button?* by Karen Katz

● In *Where Is Baby's Belly Button?* each page is a question. Raise your voice at the end of the question, pause, and wait for a response. This supports talking and understanding oral language.

● This book is fun to add props to—there are common items in the book that children are familiar with. For example, use a hat to cover your eyes or the baby's eyes. You might ask, "Where are baby's eyes?" Pause, then answer, "Under her hat!" You can do this while reading or later as a follow-up activity. This supports play and the development of background knowledge.

● This book also focuses on body parts. Call attention to children's own body parts. You might say, "There is the baby's mouth, behind the cup." Point to the picture. Then say, "Sarah, mouth. Where is your mouth?" Pause for a response. Then say, "That's right—there is your mouth. You have two lips on your mouth." This supports the development of talk, background knowledge, and vocabulary.

● The ending of this book naturally leads to a fun game of peekaboo. Have a blanket or cloth ready, cover baby's face, and ask, "Where is Sarah?" Remove the cloth, saying, "There you are!" This supports play and the development of background knowledge.

Texture Books

Texture or touch-and-feel books offer sensory experiences for children. Reading aloud to children and exposing them to all kinds of books from birth directly involves the senses of touch, sound, taste, and sight. Touch-and-feel books are specifically designed to emphasize touch, sight, and sound.

Boynton, Sandra. 1998. *Dinosaur's Binkit.* New York: Little Simon.

> This book is a combo—flaps and texture! The topic, bedtime, is a familiar one to toddlers. Although toddlers do not go to bed while in child care, they can certainly have a conversation with you about what they do at home when they get ready for bed. This book can also be related to their rest time while in your class.

Boynton, Sandra. 2003. *Fuzzy Fuzzy Fuzzy!* New York: Little Simon.

> In classic Boynton style, the animals in this book do not disappoint. The interesting, descriptive words will keep you and the children laughing. Explain or give synonyms for words the children may not be familiar with.

Bugbird, Tim. 2008. *Perfect Pets Peek-a-Boo!* Berkhamsted, UK: Make Believe Ideas.

> This Busy Baby series includes other titles such as *Friendly Farm*, *Baby Animals*, and *Wacky Wild*. In this book, children are encouraged to guess the name of the animal—not the type of animal but its actual name. This offers the opportunity to begin to teach that not all furry four-legged animals are dogs and not all dogs are named Spot.

DK Publishing. 2012. *Fluffy Animals.* New York: Dorling Kindersley.

> This Baby Touch and Feel series has padded covers for little hands to grab and carry. This large series includes other titles such as *Puppies and Kittens*, *Colors and Shapes*, *Mealtime*, *First Words*, and *Animals*. These books offer experiences that adults and children will want to repeat again and again.

Van Fleet, Matthew. 2013. *Lick!* New York: Simon and Schuster.

> Van Fleet has created a fun interactive book with rhyming text that is all about rough, slick, and sticky tongues. The oversized pull tabs are easy to manipulate.

Watt, Fiona. 2004. *That's Not My Car . . .* London, UK: Usborne.

> This title is part of the Usborne Touchy-Feely series. Additional titles include *That's Not My Puppy . . .*, *That's Not My Truck . . .*, *That's Not My Monkey . . .*, and *That's Not My Train . . .*. These books are filled with descriptive words to introduce to young children.

How to Read It: *That's Not My Car . . .* by Fiona Watt

This series of touchy-feely books are aimed at catching the attention of very young children with bright pictures and patches of different textures. They are designed to develop sensory and language awareness.

- The story actually begins on the cover. Be careful not to miss the line under the picture: "Its windows are too shiny." This supports talking and print awareness.

- With older toddlers, point out the mouse on the cover. They will quickly learn to look for the mouse on each page. Add a mouse finger puppet to help you tell the story and read the book. This will support reading and the background knowledge of narrative skills.
- Encourage, but don't force, children to touch each texture. With infants you can assist them by placing their hands on the texture. Describe the texture as they feel it. As they gain more control and eye-hand coordination, children will touch the textures on their own and will use more fine-motor skills to touch with their finger or fingers. This supports talking and background knowledge.
- Add voice inflection to emphasize the descriptive words. For example, for *smooth* make your voice smooth and draw the word out. For *rough* make your voice sound scratchy. For *lumpy* and *bumpy* exaggerate the words to make them sound "b-u-u-u-m-p-y." This supports talking and vocabulary development.
- Add more information and comparisons or contrasts while reading. You might say, "Its hubcaps are too lumpy, and its radiator is too bumpy. Lumpy and bumpy feel alike." This supports talking, vocabulary development, and background knowledge.
- Include items that children are familiar with to compare textures. You could have textured toys available in the classroom to show them that the same textures in the book are on other items, such as blocks, dolls, cars, and so on. This supports play and background knowledge.
- Throughout the day, reuse the texture words from the book. You could say, "This zipper on your jacket is rough, just like the door in the book." This supports talking, background knowledge, and vocabulary development.

Special-Feature Books

Around four to five months, infants begin to learn simple cause and effect—one event brings about another. Books that do something such as pop up or reveal a picture when a tab is moved are one more way to excite children about books, increase their attention to a story or book, or otherwise keep them engaged in learning experiences.

Clever Factory. 2010. *The Littlest Turtle.* Nashville, TN: The Clever Factory.

These books have the puppet built right in—they are definitely built to play with! The Clever Factory has produced a series of interactive books including *The Littlest Kitten, The Littlest Mouse, The Littlest Bear, The Littlest Duckling,* and *The Littlest Puppy.*

DK Publishing. 2013. *Pop-Up Peekaboo! Woof! Woof!* New York: Dorling Kindersley.

Another charming series from DK Publishing, these additional titles to the Peekaboo set include pop-up pages, which offer a whole new experience to reading. Additional titles in the series include *Bedtime, Farm, Things that Go,* and *Colors.* As with all pop-up or pop-out books, these may be ones that you will need to set aside for use when you can interact one-on-one with a child. Due to the nature of their design, they will tear easily.

Martin, Jr., Bill, and Eric Carle. 1996. *Brown Bear, Brown Bear, What Do You See?* New York: Henry Holt.

This well-known classic children's book has now been formatted in an interactive design with slide tabs. You may have already read this book many times; you and the children may even have it memorized. Use the pull tabs to make it a peekaboo guessing game.

Powers, Amelia. 2007. *Giant Pop-Out Vehicles.* San Francisco, CA: Chronicle.

Powers and Chronicle Books have created A Pop-Out Surprise Book series, which includes *Giant Pop-Out Ocean, Giant Pop-Out Safari*, and *Giant Pop-Out Shapes*, to name a few. Lifting the flaps offers a big surprise, not just a picture: the objects do pop out, adding to the excitement of reading these books.

Prince, April Jones. 2013. *Dig In!* New York: Harry N. Abrams.

These hardworking mice will intrigue children as they try to guess what the mice are building. With moving parts, this becomes a guessing, playing, and fun book. Older toddlers can use the clues to help them with their predicting skills.

Van Fleet, Matthew. 2010. *Heads.* New York: Simon and Schuster.

This book and its companion, *Tails*, cover animals from one end to the other. The short rhyming text makes it a fun read and with tabs, flaps, and texture to keep the learning going with a new experience on each page.

Yoon, Salina. 2009. *Find My Feet!* New York: Robin Corey.

A book that's a game? Six very cute animals are missing their feet. A turning wheel at the bottom of the page helps children match the feet to the correct animal. Remember to add more information about the animals while you read this book and play the game.

How to Read It: *Brown Bear, Brown Bear, What Do You See?* by Bill Martin, Jr., and Eric Carle

This well-loved classic children's book is now an interactive board book. Many children learn to "read" this book very early on because of its rhyming text and predictable pattern. The red bird always comes after the brown bear, and the yellow duck always comes after the red bird. By adding the slide tabs, the picture of the next animal is revealed in a box after reading the text. As children become familiar with the story, they can confidently say the next animal even before the tab is moved.

- The repetition of "What do you see?" prompts children to provide the answer. They will learn quickly which animal comes next. Raise the pitch of your voice at the end of the question to indicate that they are to respond. Pause and wait for a response. If the children guess incorrectly, be positive. You can guide them to the correct answer, saying for example, "There is a blue horse in this book, but that comes later. Next is the green frog." This supports talking, vocabulary development, and background knowledge.

- Make comparisons between the small picture of the animal under the tab and the larger picture on the following page. You could say, "This is a small blue horse." Then turn the page and say, "And this is a much bigger picture of a blue horse." This supports talking and background knowledge.

- Add puppets or other props to this book. The animals may not be the same colors, but you can make connections between the pictures in the book to a puppet, real photograph, or toy. You can say, "I see a white dog looking at me. Here is a picture of a brown dog. He is playing with a ball." This supports talking, vocabulary development, and background knowledge.
- As with any book that has animals in it, you can include the animal's sound when you are reading. You can say, "This is the green frog. A frog says, 'Ribbit-ribbit.'" This supports talking and phonological awareness.

I Can Do It! Books

These books do not have flaps, tabs, or texture, but they are not short on interaction. The play comes from doing what the babies or animals are doing in the books. Imitating what you see in the books gives you and the children opportunities to play with these books as well as read them. They are not your ordinary sit-down-and-listen books.

Boynton, Sandra. 2008. *Let's Dance, Little Pookie*. New York: Robin Corey.

Reading Boynton's *Let's Dance, Little Pookie* is really a singing and dancing fest. The movements are just what toddlers love to do—hop, march, reach up so high, and bend down so low. If you are reading this to an infant, the rhythm of your voice will keep their attention as you read. You can move his legs and arms to show him the movements. Remember to make sure baby is happy with the movements. Watch for signs of distress, and leave the movements out if baby is not having fun.

Carle, Eric. 1999. *From Head to Toe*. New York: HarperFestival.

Young ones may enjoy hearing this book and looking at the illustrations; however, once they can begin to imitate the movements, they will be turning, twisting, and wiggling through the entire story. The repeated line, "I can do it!" helps children as they master new movements.

Cronin, Doreen. 2007. *Bounce*. New York: Atheneum.

Plan to move when you read this and its companion book, *Wiggle*, to toddlers. The rhyming text lets you read with lots of emphasis while you lead children wiggling and bouncing through the stories. These books have hard covers with paper pages. If the children in your class are not yet ready to handle paper pages, keep these books away from little hands until you can read with the children.

Hutton, John. 2013. *Blocks*. Cincinnati, OH: Blue Manatee.

Hutton's Baby Unplugged series includes titles to encourage children to discover the world around them. Other titles in the series are *Yard, Ball, Blanket*, and *Pets*. When reading *Blocks*, you do not have to sit and read. Get out the blocks, build, play, and read!

Katz, Karen. 2011. *Ten Tiny Babies*. New York: Little Simon.

Katz's cute, active babies are back in this title that is available with a hard cover or as a board book. The rhyming book covers activities familiar to babies and toddlers. They may just want to get up and spin, bang, shout, and hop right along with the story.

Oxenbury, Helen. 1999. *Clap Hands*. New York: Little Simon.

> This set of four board books includes *All Fall Down, Clap Hands, Say Goodnight,* and *Tickle, Tickle*. The rhyming text gives an easy rhythm for reading. This series includes very familiar actions and activities that babies can imitate.

Smith, Charles, Jr. 2008. *Dance with Me*. Somerville, MA: Candlewick Press.

> Super Sturdy Picture Books are a good transition style as children begin to move from board books. For younger ones who are not ready yet, you can help them with the book while you are reading and dancing. *Dance with Me* includes moves that toddlers can do.

Ziefert, Harriet. 2011. *Wiggle! Like an Octopus*. Maplewood, NJ: Blue Apple.

> This sturdy board book will have toddlers wiggling, waddling, and swooping as you read the rhythmic text about animals taking a dip in the sea.

How to Read It: *Clap Hands* by Helen Oxenbury

This book is full of babies doing what babies do. They move, eat, drink, clap, play, and gesture. The book has a nice size to read to children, but they can also handle it themselves since it is a sturdy board-book design.

- Talk with the children about what the babies are doing in the book. Ask questions and describe their actions. Remember to give children a chance to respond. Having conversations about books helps children build oral language skills and teaches that conversations have a pattern: speak and listen.

- Make sure there is space in the room for babies to move freely. Encourage children who may mimic actions from the book, such as "dance and spin," or you can dance and spin with them. Make sure that the baby is enjoying the activity, and change to a slower, calmer activity if a baby shows distress. This supports play and background knowledge.

- By about ten months of age, children may begin to wave goodbye. At appropriate times, such as when a parent is leaving, wave goodbye, say the word, and encourage children to imitate. This helps children develop gestures that help them communicate, even before they have the vocabulary.

- When you are feeding children, repeat the line from the book, "Open wide and pop it in." Make up more rhyming lines during routine times of the day. For example, you can say, "Change your diaper to keep you dry. Nice and clean so you won't cry." Rhyme and rhythm keep children's attention, and narrating what you are doing through the day helps children build vocabulary. This supports talking, vocabulary development, and phonological awareness.

Interactive Story Time with Infants

We use the term *story time* very loosely when talking about infants. Reading books with infants should be informal and should happen throughout the day.

- While you are rocking a baby—Sing a song that has hand movements, read a book with flaps, then play peekaboo.
- While you are on the floor playing with a couple of children—Say a rhyme and include gestures, open a texture book on the floor, encourage children to touch the textures, read the book and talk about the different textures, and then sing another song.
- Gather a small group of children (who are interested) in the book area—Sing a song, read a book, and sing another song.

As you know, their attention spans are short. That's okay! Do not worry if some of these story times are only a minute long with the youngest children. Use your voice, make eye contact, and take your cue from what they are looking at.

Even though these times may be very short, be prepared and plan your book-sharing and literacy activities with infants. Use the story-time planning tools in Chapter 6. Your plan will not include as many items when you are planning for infants; however, having a plan will help keep you on track with what you want to accomplish with the children in your class. You can also use the sample story times provided; just modify them to fit the age and interest level of the children in your class.

Tips for Successful Story Times

- Pick times of day when the children are rested.
- Allow the children to pat and chew on the books.
- Encourage babies to touch the textures in the books. You may need to help them by guiding their hands to the parts of the page.
- Repeat reading books that they show interest in.
- Use a high-pitched voice, and say words slowly and clearly to get a child's attention.
- Look at and talk about the pictures.
- Allow children time to respond or imitate, even if they are not verbal yet.
- Choose books about things that children are familiar with.
- Point out words in books and in the environment.
- Lay a book on the floor and face the baby while you are reading. The text will be upside down for you, but you can watch to see where baby is looking.
- Follow the baby's lead and interest, and talk about what she is looking at.

Don't have an interactive book handy or the titles we've suggested? You can make any book interactive even if it does not have built-in features such as flaps, tabs, or moving parts. You can use the techniques we have suggested with just about any book. Be creative and have fun! Here are a few suggestions for making reading times more interactive:

- Add a puppet as you read the book.
- Add a prop that is mentioned in the book.
- Sing the book or add a song.
- Lift-the-flap books are essentially playing peekaboo in book form. Open and close any book while you are reading to encourage children's curiosity and keep them guessing.
- Use a cloth to cover a book or toy and encourage children to look under and behind.
- As you read any book, ask *what* questions, allow time for the child to respond, and then answer the question. Give time for the child to repeat the word. For a baby this may be a babble or coo.
- Even when there are just a couple of words on the page, add your own knowledge and experiences to the picture. Talk about experiences the child may have had as well.
- Use your voice. Add excitement by changing your voice, making it loud or soft, high or low, squeaky, rough, scratchy, deep, or whispery.
- Do what they are doing in the book. If they are shaking their hips, demonstrate for the children and encourage them to shake their hips. If the characters are marching, show the children how to march, describe how to do it, then encourage them to march. For very young ones, help them. Lift their arms for "reach to the sky" or move their feet for "running so fast." Remember, any time you are doing actions with an infant, watch for cues that the child is enjoying it. At any sign of distress, change activities.

Interactive Story Time with Older Toddlers and Twos

As children get older and their attention spans lengthen, you can begin to have a more formal story time with the class. Of course, before they are mobile you have a captive audience, so you can read and sing to them and they cannot wander off. Once they are mobile, it may be like trying to read to a moving target. That is okay. Even if they wander off, you can keep reading to the children who remain. The "wanderer" is most likely still listening and may rejoin the group. Initially, your story time may only last about five minutes, but as toddlers grow you will be able to keep their attention for longer periods of time.

Young children will be done with a book, song, or story time before you are. That does not mean you are not doing it "right." They are very busy! They have a lot to pay attention to. Expect that they will wander in and out of story time. There are so many possibilities of ways to share books interactively with young children, both one-on-one and in small groups and using different types of books and different ways of sharing the same book. The wonderful thing is that you are with the children every day. You see them grow, know their interests, and can build on their need for repetition while adding new elements to their learning. Share your enjoyment and they will also learn to enjoy, which will later help them as they learn to read.

A Flippy-Flappy, Touchy-Feely Story Time

This is a sample story-time model. Choices of books, songs, rhymes, and fingerplays should be based on your preferences and those of the children in the class. Consider the children's ages, likes and dislikes, attention spans, and developmental levels. This sample includes more stories and activities than young children will typically have the attention span for. Pick and choose your favorites; always plan for more and adjust as needed. Watch their cues and stop when needed to avoid frustration and behavior issues. There will be days when they are ready for more. Story times for infants and toddlers should include more songs, chants, and fingerplays than books to keep their attention. Include in your newsletters, daily notes, or posts by the door information for parents and families about what you are reading and singing with the children.

● Use the same song to transition into your story time each time. Singing helps support phonological awareness. Using the same song each time helps establish routine; the children will learn very quickly that this cue means that books are next. Try the following song, or any song that you like.

Peekaboo

(Sing to the tune of "Frère Jacques")

Peekaboo, peekaboo (cover face with hands two times)

I see you! I see you! (point to children)

I see your button nose. (point to nose)

I see your tiny toes. (point to toes)

I see you! Peekaboo! (cover face with hands two times)

Repeat two times, and clap together.

- Offer a description of the theme. Keep this very short and concise: "Today we have some books about pets," or simply say, "It's story time!"

- Sing a song related to the theme. Singing is fun! Do not worry if you do not have perfect pitch. In songs, each syllable has a different note, and the children hear words broken into parts. This phonological awareness will help them when they have to sound out words. You can write the lyrics on a whiteboard or sheet of paper and point to them as you sing. This visual aid helps develop print awareness as the children make the connection between the written words and the lyrics.

Where Has My Little Dog Gone?

Oh where, oh where has my little dog gone? (shade eyes, look around)

Oh where, oh where can he be?

With his ears so short (touch ears)

And his tail so long (wag hand behind back)

Oh where, oh where can he be?

- Read a book related to the theme, such as *Perfect Pets Peek-a-Boo!* by Tim Bugbird. As you read the text, use your voice to emphasize the rhyming words. If the book is a bit long for your group, shorten it as you need to in order to keep their attention. The bright, colorful pictures and the touch-and-feel parts will help keep them engaged. Give the children the chance to feel the textures, and describe what they are feeling: *fuzzy, smooth, soft, furry,* and *squishy.* The flaps give opportunities for you to ask, "What's under there?"

- Sing another song or chant related to the theme, such as the following. By adding movement to songs, young children can use their whole bodies. This helps them internalize and understand what is happening. It is also a lot of fun and will capture their attention. You can also add a dog puppet to the song to really engage the children.

Wags

My favorite puppy's name is Wags.

He eats so much that his tummy sags. (hold tummy)

His ears flip-flop and his tail wig-wags. (wave hands by ears, then hand behind back)

And when he walks, he zigs and zags. (move body side to side)

He goes flip-flop, wig-wag, zigzag. (wave hands by ears, then hand behind back, move body side to side)

I love Wags, and he loves me.

- Read a book related to the theme, such as *Baby Pets!* by DK Publishing. Each page is a question. Raise the pitch of your voice at the end of each question to cue the children that you expect a response. The tabs on this book extend from the page, which makes it easier for small fingers to help lift them. This book is full of descriptive words, such as *stripy, fluffy, shiny, scaly, bright,* and *chirpy.*

- Do a fingerplay, song, or rhyme, such as "These Are Baby's Fingers." Use movement and suit the actions to the words.

  These Are Baby's Fingers

  These are baby's fingers, (wiggle fingers)

  And these are baby's toes. (wiggle toes)

  This is baby's belly button. (circle finger on baby's tummy)

  'Round and 'round it goes.

  These are baby's eyes, (gently touch eyes)

  And this is baby's nose. (touch nose)

  This is baby's belly button (tickle tummy)

  Right where (your name) *blows!* (buzz lips on baby's tummy)

- Read a book related to the theme, such as *Who's in the Forest?* by Phillis Gershator. This die-cut book gives you the chance to peek through the holes to see what creatures are hiding in the forest. You can add rhythm to the rhyming text to keep children's interest. Encourage them to look through the holes and find the next animal.

- Just as with an opening song, singing the same closing song at the end of each story time signals to the children that story time is over. This song offers a smooth transition into the next activity. Sing the following song or any song you like.

  Story time is over now.

  Story time is over now, over now, over now.

  Story time is over now.

  It's time to (fill in the blank with the next activity).

Chapter 3

Books That Rock!

What's the Connection?

- Practice: Sing
- Component: Phonological Awareness
- Focus:
    - Rhythm and Rhyme
    - Action and Movement

Books are written and illustrated to be read. The fun thing about children's books is that many of them are written to be sung. Some are very obvious: just by looking at the title, you know it is a song. Often, they are standard children's classics, and you can either read the book or sing it. Some books will have a note on the front instructing you to download the song or it comes with a CD. There are other books that take a little detective work and creativity to sing. There is no rule that says you cannot sing any book you want. If the text has a rhythm that lends itself to singing, go ahead. You can add a new experience to a book children have heard many times by adding a tune to it. Some classic nursery rhymes, such as "Humpty Dumpty," "Mary Had a Little Lamb," and "Jack and Jill," began as rhymes but have evolved into familiar songs.

Often there are clues on the inside flap or back cover of a book that let you know the book can be sung or read in a rhythmic singsong way. Look for descriptions such as *rhythmic text* or *lyrical prose*, where the words in the title are also repeated in a rhythmic way throughout the book. These phrases let you know that there is an intended rhythm.

> **TIP**
>
> Children love singing, whether they are listening to you sing or they are learning the words and can begin to join in.

What to Look For

- Songs that children are familiar with
- Books that include the actions to go along with the songs
- Books with the musical score included
- Books with an accompanying music CD
- Classic Mother Goose rhymes
- Books that include newer original rhymes and poems
- Books that have rhymes and songs in children's native languages

Singing songs with and to children especially supports two areas of early literacy: *vocabulary*—knowing the meanings of words—and *phonological awareness*—hearing and playing with the smaller sounds in words. Although singing may be a simple activity that you do every day with the children, there is a lot that is happening when you sing. Songs have new words in them. For babies, just hearing or being exposed to the words is good. For toddlers, you may explain some words but not all. There is no need to turn this into an extremely structured activity; remember to have fun. In songs, there is a distinct note for each syllable. This helps children hear the syllables more clearly, which will help them later as they sound out words when they learn to read. Singing slows down the pronunciation of words, making it easier for children to hear both the sounds of words and the lilt of the language. Add actions and movements to the songs; this helps children learn and remember the words.

What You Can Do with Rhyming and Lyrical Books

Singing books and using rhymes are great ways to help build skills that infants and toddlers need, as well to encourage their love of books, reading, and stories. Books you can sing, that rhyme, or that have lyrical text are most closely tied to the practice of singing; however, these types of books can be used in all of the practices that support children's growth and development.

Sing

Singing slows down language. It takes us longer to sing a rhyme than to say it. Children can hear the sounds of language more easily when we sing. Also, there is a distinct note for each syllable, so children hear words broken down into parts, which will help them later sound out words when they learn to read. All of these aspects of singing begin developing very early in children; they are part of phonological awareness. It is important to sing with children from a very early age. Not only do children enjoy songs and singing, they are building very important skills that they will later use when learning how to read.

You can sing just about any book for infants and toddlers. The text is short, so you can add a little rhythm to your voice and make it a song. Babies pay attention when you sing and also hear distinct notes for the syllables in words. Even books that only have one word on each page can be turned into a fun tune. For example, if a book has a picture of a ball and the only text is *ball*, you can point to the ball and sing, "That is a red ball, red ball, red ball. That is a red ball, and it is round!" In this example you not only read it with rhythm, which will capture children's attention, you also emphasize syllables, add more information to the book, reinforce colors and shapes, and make the reading a bit more fun.

Songs and rhymes often have interesting words that we do not hear in regular conversation. Include singing and rhyming throughout the day by pairing them with a book that you read, singing a book instead of reading it, transitioning from one activity to another, and during daily activities such as cleaning up or washing hands. This helps build children's vocabulary. For example, if the toddlers are washing their hands, you can sing a tune that includes words such as *scrub*, *lather*, and *rinse*. Children often respond to singing, and it makes activities more fun.

Singing songs with babies and toddlers helps them hear words being broken into smaller sounds. Reading a book sounds different than singing it does. Singing naturally slows down and emphasizes the pronunciation of words. Try this: First, say the words to "Twinkle, Twinkle, Little Star" as if you are reciting a poem. Next, read a book version of *Twinkle, Twinkle, Little Star*. Then, sing the song. Do you hear a difference in the rhythm and speed?

To reinforce ideas, themes, and concepts, sing a song or rhyme and then repeat it with a book. For example, after singing "The More We Get Together," read the book, describe the pictures, and talk about what the friends in the book are doing. Combining books and singing helps build background knowledge and supports vocabulary development.

Nursery rhymes are fun to sing, say, and read. A 2011 study by L. J. Harper in the *Journal of Language and Literacy Education* says that young children who learn nursery rhymes have stronger phonological skills than those who do not. Because of the rhythm and rhyme, nursery rhymes help children develop the ability to play with parts of words. Learn the rhymes or songs that families say or sing with their children, and make a book of their rhymes and songs. Incorporate rhymes throughout the day through books, flannel-board stories, or chanting and reciting. As with any activity you may be doing with the children, if you see that they are on overload and singing is not helping, then sing another time.

Family Connection

Whenever you introduce a new song to the children in your class, make sure you let parents and families know the words. Let them know that they can help reinforce the song at home. Encourage families to sing with their children a lot. Tell parents that when they sing to their babies or toddlers, singing slows down the pronunciation of words and makes each part of a word easier for children to hear. This helps children learn new words and to hear the sounds in words—phonological awareness. Also, remind families that singing and saying rhymes in their native languages is important. This will help children when they start to learn how to read.

Read

Although it may seem contradictory to talk about the practice of reading while focusing on singing, the two practices support each other. Many of the skills children develop through singing will carry over to reading. For instance, children need to learn how to handle books and develop print awareness. When you are singing a book, it is a great way to allow young ones to practice their page-turning skills. It does not matter if they keep up with you; you know the words.

Reading and singing are both great ways to build a child's vocabulary and expose them to rich language. The repetition of singing and reading is extremely important for infants and toddlers. By adding a book that can be sung, you can repeat the words to the song while reading it or show the pictures while you sing it. Have fun with rhyming books and books you can sing. Young children are just beginning to build relationships with books and reading. If you are having fun, they will, too.

Family Connection

Provide parents with a list of good age-appropriate books that can be sung. Check with your local library; they may have book lists available or can suggest books to go on the list. Include information for families about reading and singing. For example, you could write on the list, "Sing and read favorite songs with your children. This will help strengthen their ability to hear smaller sounds in words. This is called *phonological awareness*, a skill that will help your child when she is learning to read later on." Also, encourage families to write the words to songs they enjoy singing to their children and make their own books. The songs can be in any language.

Talk

Babies begin using gestures very early, before they can talk. Gestures are a young child's language. By adding gestures, actions, and movements to songs and books, you can teach children communication tools. Watch for a baby's cues. As you build relationships with the children in your class, you will begin to learn what their cues and gestures mean. They may wiggle their fingers for the star in "Twinkle, Twinkle, Little Star" or move their arms side to side to wash the spider out in "The Itsy Bitsy Spider." Respond to their cues and gestures, ask questions, or describe what they are doing. You can say, "I see you moving your fingers like the twinkling stars. Is that what you want to sing about?" Pause for a response, even if it is just babbling, cooing, or more gestures. Then sing the song. When you respond to a young child's gestures, add words and description. Children benefit from rich language and hearing more words. For example, a child may bounce on your lap for "Five Little Monkeys Jumping on the Bed." Respond to his gestures. You can say, "You are bouncy today, like the monkeys jumping on the bed. Do you want to sing 'Five Little Monkeys Jumping on the Bed'?" Give the child time to respond, even if it is just babbling. By using the word *bouncy* for *jumping*, you are adding to the child's vocabulary. Sing the song or get the book and sing while you read. By responding to the child's gestures, you are help him build language and vocabulary skills.

Add flannel-board stories or story gloves to books you can sing. Additional elements give children more to look at and more for you to talk about. Use descriptive words and narrate what you are doing. You can say, "Now I'm putting the sun up. It will dry up all of the rain." With toddlers you can allow them to help with the flannel pieces. This will help keep them engaged and actively involved in singing the song or saying the rhyme. Remember to keep up your narration. You can say, "Alden is putting up the bed that the monkeys will jump on."

Family Connection

Encourage parents to use the gestures that go with songs. Show them books that include the actions to songs, and demonstrate the gestures that you have been doing with their children. Let them know that families who use a lot of gestures when they communicate with their children will see their babies' language increase at a more rapid rate than those who do not use a lot of gestures.

Write

To be able to learn to write, children need to develop the fine-motor skills needed to hold a pencil or other writing utensil. By adding actions and finger movements to songs, you are helping them build eye-hand coordination and the dexterity they will need for writing when they are older. Every time they wiggle their fingers to twinkle the stars or crawl the spider up the spout, they are gaining more and more control over their fingers and hands.

It is important for children to learn that print represents sounds and words. Letters do not mean much to a baby or toddler; they are simply squiggles on a page. However, seeing the words to a song they know printed on the page begins to teach children that those lines and squiggles represent sounds and words. Write out the lyrics to favorite songs on large paper or a whiteboard. The website http://www.earlylit.net/storytime-resources/ is a good resource for common children's songs. The printable pages can be displayed, or you can cut and paste them to make a handout for parents (just change the font size). Helping children make connections between written and spoken words supports development of print awareness and letter knowledge.

Family Connection

After writing out the words to songs on large paper or a whiteboard, leave them up for parents to see when they pick up and drop off their children. Draw attention to the board either through a note on the door, in a newsletter, or on a daily sheet. Give families the words and actions to the songs, and let them know that using arm and finger movements helps children develop eye-hand coordination and dexterity that will help them learn to write when they are older.

Play

Because children love to play and also enjoy singing and music, these practices work very well together. With a little creativity and a few props, you can help children build important skills every day. While you are singing a book, give each child a shaker or bells so they can make music along with you. This makes singing a sensorimotor activity, which helps them begin to learn rhythms. Keep child-safe musical instruments available on a low shelf for children to explore. When a child initiates making music, sing along. This makes it fun for them because they are in control of the rhythm. Aside from using musical instruments, you can also have puppets and stuffed animals available. Demonstrate the actions to a song with them; as children get older they will move the puppet or animal along with the song or book. For example, have a stuffed monkey jump up and down while you sing "Five Little Monkeys Jumping on the Bed." The more fun they have singing, making music, and adding movements, the more fun children will have when you sing books, which builds excitement about reading and print motivation. Another way to play with songs and rhymes is to act them out. This type of activity can be very fun for older toddlers. Make sure to select songs that all children can have a chance to participate in if they want, such as "Five Little Monkeys" or "The Farmer in the Dell."

Throughout the day, encourage children to choose books on their own. When you are selecting a book, keep them engaged and involved. By building their interest in the book you are going to read or sing, you build excitement about reading. One way to do this is to create a game out of selecting song books to read and sing. When you sing, set the book upright so they can see the cover. For infants and very young toddlers you can say, "This is a farmer. What song do we know about a farmer?" Pause to give them time to respond. "I know, Old MacDonald had a farm with a lot of animals on it. We have that book about him. Here it is! Let's sing about all of the animals he had." With older, more verbal children, you can encourage them to guess what song you are going to sing by looking at the book cover or picture. When they guess or predict, they are developing narrative skills and background knowledge.

- Put a few books in a bag, and draw one out then sing the song. You can encourage older toddlers to guess what song it is by looking at the cover of the book.
- Print and cut out pictures that represent songs to put in a song bag. Pull out a picture, then sing that song.
- Make a song cube to select songs to sing. Use a small box or large block, and tape pictures that represent songs or rhymes on each side of the cube. Roll the cube and sing the song that is facing up when it stops.

Family Connection

Remind parents that when their babies play with the pots and pans and make music, they are helping build literacy skills. Encourage families to sing along when their child makes up a rhythm, even if they are singing nonsense words. This helps children get excited about singing and reading.

You can sing just about any book, even if it was not written to go along with a song. Use the techniques we have suggested. You can also add rhymes or rhyming words to books. Be creative and have fun! Here are a few suggestions to incorporate singing into reading a book:

- Sing a song that is related to the book after you have read it.
- Read rhymes and poems.
- Bounce babies to rhythms and syllables in words.
- Clap out syllables when saying children's names.
- Add a rhyming word to pictures in books or to books that may only have one word on a page, labeling the object in the picture.

A few notes about singing with young children: Pay attention to the complexity of a song or rhyme. Repetitive songs and verses are easier for young children than ones that do not repeat.

Some songs repeat in each line, some repeat verses, some have only a common chorus, and some do not repeat at all. If there is no repetition in a song, you will need to repeat it several times for children to begin to learn it. "Zipper songs" allow most of the song structure and words to stay the same while changing out one word, phrase, or sound—"Old MacDonald Had a Farm" is a good example. Zipper songs support grammar, sentence structure, and cognitive thinking because the same type or category of word is substituted. "Piggyback songs" put new words to the tune of a familiar song. Piggyback songs are harder for young children than zipper songs because the tune is the same but the words are different.

Classic or Traditional Song Books

Many classic children's songs and nursery rhymes have been adapted into books. This is by no means an exhaustive list but provides just a few examples of books that are available. If you or the children in your classroom have a favorite song, check to see if there is a book available. Also, given the popularity of many of these songs and rhymes, there is a variety among authors and formats. The same song in different forms—board book, picture book, big book—and with different illustrators can offer new experiences for children.

Christelow, Eileen. 2012. *Five Little Monkeys Jumping on the Bed*. Boston, MA: HMH Books for Young Readers.

> This book adds a bit of story to the familiar fingerplay and song. Children quickly learn the repeated line, "No more monkeys jumping on the bed!" Christelow adds a twist to the end when mother monkey goes to bed . . . and jumps! Reading this book is a great addition to literacy activities when children are already familiar with the song. With very young ones who may not have the attention to last through five verses, start with "Three little monkeys jumping on the bed."

Church, Caroline Jayne. 2002. *Do Your Ears Hang Low?* Frome, Somerset, UK: Chicken House.

> This version of the familiar children's song is actually a love story between two puppies. The book ends with an exciting surprise fold out. This story is a bit long, so be patient if younger ones are not ready to listen to the whole book. Dorothea Deprisco Wang offers a version of this story with slide tabs.

Church, Caroline Jayne. 2011. *The More We Get Together*. New York: Cartwheel.

> This classic song has been sung in early childhood classrooms for years. Church adds simple, clear, colorful illustrations to this children's favorite.

Kubler, Annie. 2002. *Head, Shoulders, Knees, and Toes*. Sydney, Aus.: Child's Play International.

> Kubler's version of this classic includes her familiar babies from different ethnic groups. This title is available in many languages. Additional versions are available by Nicola Baxter, Zita Newcome, and Mike Wohnoutka.

Kubler, Annie. 2001. *If You're Happy and You Know It. . ..* Sydney, Aus.: Child's Play International.

> Kubler's series of familiar songs and rhymes has been specifically designed for babies. This book is a good introduction to well-known nursery rhymes and interactive text. This board-book version includes musical notation. Additional versions are available by Jane Cabrera and David Carter.

Kubler, Annie. 2003. *Row, Row, Row Your Boat*. Sydney, Aus.: Child's Play International.

> This board book is delightful and full of colorful and interesting pictures. Most children learn this song young, and the diverse babies in this version will draw the attention of even the youngest in your class. Kubler's version includes additional verses. Additional versions are available by Jane Cabrera, Iza Trapani, and Lara Ede.

Raffi. 1997. *Baby Beluga*. New York: Crown Books for Young Readers.

> This title in the Raffi Songs to Read series is a great addition to any classroom library. If you do not know the Raffi tune, don't worry. The rhythm of the text is easy to sing to any tune you feel comfortable with.

Reasoner, Charles. 2013. *Twinkle, Twinkle, Little Star*. North Makato, MN: Capstone.

> This version of *Twinkle, Twinkle, Little Star* has charming illustrations to spark young children's interest. Additional versions are available by Iza Trapani, Jane Cabrera, Caroline Jayne Church, Rosemary Wells, Sanja Rescek, and Jerry Pinkney.

Siomades, Lorianne. 2001. *The Itsy Bitsy Spider*. Honesdale, PA: Boyds Mills.

> This very popular and well-loved children's rhyme can be read, recited, or sung. The delightful illustrations in Siomades's version include vivid illustrations that will capture

children's attention. The book is hardcover, which is great for teacher use, and the pictures are larger than in typical board books. This makes them easier to see if you are reading to more than a couple of children at a time. Additional versions are available by Rosemary Wells, Jeanette Winter, Iza Trapani, Annie Kubler, Nora Hilb, and Little Learners.

Smath, Jerry. 1991. *The Wheels on the Bus*. New York: Grosset and Dunlap.

This is a very noisy bus ride! This book to sing includes active and sparkling words as well as vivid interesting illustrations. This pudgy board book is small and easy for little hands to hold. To read with more than one or two children at a time, look for a larger version so they can all see the pictures easily. Additional versions are available by Raffi, Annie Kubler, Jane Cabrera, and Lara Ede.

Wells, Rosemary. 1998. *Old MacDonald*. New York: Scholastic.

This title is part of Rosemary Wells's Read to Your Bunny Very First Library collection. Her version of this familiar song is quite simple, with the story focusing on a duck. Pictures and animal sounds for chicken, goose, cow, pig, donkey, dog, and sheep are included. Additional versions are available by Salina Yoon, Child's Play, Jill Ackerman, Jane Cabrera, and Little Learners.

How to Read It: *The Itsy Bitsy Spider*

This classic nursery rhyme has been sung and recited for generations. It is a good example of a familiar song that can grow with children from infancy and has been adapted into a variety of books.

- With a very young infant, you can just sing. If you like, you can do movements *on* the baby. As children become a little older you can start by moving their hands, then have them move their own hands, and ultimately let them do the movements on their own. This progression is known as *scaffolding*. Simply put, the amount of assistance the adult provides depends on what the child is able to do on his own. This supports singing, playing, and phonological awareness. Here is an example of the progression:

- **With infants:**
  The itsy bitsy spider climbed up the water spout. (fingers crawl up child's arm)
  Down came the rain and washed the spider out. (flutter fingers down baby's body and then side to side)
  Out came the sun and dried up all the rain. (circle baby's face)
  And the itsy bitsy spider climbed up the spout again. (fingers crawl up body)

- **With young toddlers:**
  The itsy bitsy spider climbed up the water spout. (fingers crawl up child's body)
  Down came the rain and washed the spider out. (flutter fingers downward in the air, move arms side to side)
  Out came the sun and dried up all the rain. (circle hands over head, then with palms up, arms move up and down again)
  And the itsy bitsy spider climbed up the spout again. (move fingers up the other arm)

- **With older toddlers:**

  The itsy bitsy spider climbed up the water spout. (child makes fingers "crawl")
  Down came the rain and washed the spider out. (child flutters fingers and moves arms or hands side to side)
  Out came the sun and dried up all the rain. (child holds arms in circle overhead)
  And the itsy bitsy spider climbed up the spout again. (child makes fingers "crawl")

This book is fun and easy to add props to, such as a puppet or glove puppet. If you do not have spider and sun puppets, you can make them easily out of socks or other materials. Describe the color, texture, shape, and size of the puppet to the children to add new and descriptive words to this familiar song. This supports play, background knowledge, vocabulary, and oral language.

You can also add a flannel board or use the flannel pieces on a glove puppet. There are many ready-made flannel pieces for a board or glove available for purchase, or you can make your own. This supports play and background knowledge.

There are quite a few versions of this classic nursery rhyme as well as many other common rhymes. Look for different versions and formats to find the one you and the children like best. Here's a quick look at some similarities and differences.

Author	Format/Binding	Special Features
Rosemary Wells	Board book	Spider is joined by a cute goose and a chicken at the end. This version follows the traditional verse of the rhyme.
Jeanette Winter	Board book	Turn this book sideways to follow the spider's climbing adventure. The book is a bit smaller than standard board books, which may make it easier for little ones to carry around.
Lorianne Siomades	Hardcover	The large pictures and text make this one great for reading to a few children at a time. Bold illustrations include a colorful butterfly and an umbrella.
Iza Trapani	Hardcover	Trapani adds more verses and introduces a few more animals into the mix as the spider crawls up more than just the waterspout. She crawls all through the house and yard until finally resting in her web in the sun. This book has a good clear picture of the water spout.
Annie Kubler	Board book	This board book includes the sign language to accompany the song.
Nora Hilb	Hardcover	This book is a die-cut book with holes. The version in this peekaboo style introduces children to many of the spider's friends, such as Incy Wincy Spider and Itcy Nitchy Spider.
Little Learners	Board book	This board book comes with the finger puppet included. This version also has some lines that are different from the traditional song.

Other Books You Can Sing

Some books were written to be sung. Perhaps they are the lyrics of a traditional children's song or they have a lyrical text that is easy to transition into singing. Be aware that even though children may be familiar with the tune that a book is written to, it is more difficult for them to change the words. If, for example, they know "The Wheels on the Bus," and you read a book that is sung to the same tune, they will certainly enjoy it. But, inserting the new words is more challenging.

Alexander, Martha. 2011. *A You're Adorable*. Somerville, MA: Candlewick Press.

> What do you get when you combine an alphabet book with a 1940s hit song by Buddy Kaye, Fred Wise, and Sidney Lippman? A great book you can sing! If you do not know the tune to this oldie but goodie, the musical score is included. The multicultural illustrations of children offer opportunities to talk about what is happening in the pictures. The book gives good exposure to the alphabet. Just remember, exposure is all that is necessary at this age.

Berkes, Marianne. 2007. *Over in the Jungle: A Rainforest Rhyme*. Nevada City, CA: Dawn.

> Berkes also has written *Over in the Ocean: In a Coral Reef* and others with the same tune, "Over in the Meadow." With their clever illustrations and photographs, these books will have children counting, clapping, and singing. They come in hardcover and board-book formats. The board-book version emphasizes body movements to match the text.

Boynton, Sandra. 1982. *Moo, Baa, La La La!* New York: Little Simon.

> Boynton's silly, hilarious, and adorable animals snort and snuff, quack, neigh, and la-la-la all the way through this fun-to-read book. The rhythm of the text makes for a nice mixture between reading some pages and singing others.

Boynton, Sandra. 2010. *Perfect Piggies!* New York: Workman.

> There is no mystery about whether or not this book can be sung. It says right on the cover: "A Book! A Song! A Celebration!" Information on downloading a free copy of the song is available on the inside front cover. Not only will the children love this fun book, but also most adults really like to read it and sing it.

Cabrera, Jane. 1999. *Over in the Meadow*. New York: Scholastic.

> Cabrera's version of this traditional counting poem is easy to read with rhythm or to sing if you like. The book introduces children to a variety of animals and their familiar activities. Turtles dig, bees buzz, and worms wiggle. This version may be a little long; be aware of children if they lose interest. You do not have to read the whole book in one sitting.

Craig, Lindsey. 2012. *Dancing Feet!* New York: Knopf.

> This is actually a picture book for reading; however, the clues for singing it are on the inside flap in the description of the book. It is described as a "get-up-and-dance book—so catchy and rhythmic, you'll almost want to sing it."

Cummings, Pat. 1998. *My Aunt Came Back*. New York: HarperFestival.

> Illustrations and text come together in this rhythmic rhyming book of far-off destinations. Not necessarily written as a song, it quickly becomes singable. The seven rhymes tell of an

aunt's traveling adventures and the items she brings back to her niece. This book is full of new and interesting vocabulary for toddlers.

Hort, Lenny. 2003. *The Seals on the Bus*. New York: Square Fish.

Here's a twist on the well-known "The Wheels on the Bus" tune. Instead of going "open and shut" or "swish, swish, swish," you will "honk, honk, honk" and "baah, baah, baah" all around the town. Singing and reading this whole book may be a little long. Stop if the children are losing interest, or focus on their favorite animals and animal sounds.

Katz, Karen. 2013. *The Babies on the Bus*. New York: Henry Holt.

Katz's rendition of the favorite "The Wheels on the Bus" includes her very cute babies as they take you on a new ride with this familiar song.

Weatherford, Carol. 2006. *Jazz Baby*. New York: Lee and Low.

This book is full of rhythm, rhyme, and music. The text is easily read or sung to the tune of "Pat-a-Cake," and children can clap along and repeat the words, "Jazz Baby, Jazz Baby," which appears on each two-page spread. This book offers a nice combination of music and movement, singing and reading.

Wilson, Karma. 2005. *Bear Snores On*. New York: Little Simon.

Wilson's Bear stories are written with a distinct rhythmic quality. The classic board-books set includes *Bear Wants More*, *Bear Feels Sick*, and *Bear Feels Scared*. All of the Bear stories have endearing messages of friends helping friends. These are definitely stories to be read; however, if you practice them a few times, you will find a very nice lyrical cadence to the text. This ends up being somewhere between singing and reading, which offers a new experience for young children.

How to Read It: *Dancing Feet!* by Lindsey Craig

This is a book that was not written to the tune of a song. It is actually a picture book for reading; however, the clues for singing it are on the inside flap in the description of the book. Since this book is not written to another tune, get prepared before reading it to the class. Practice it, and find the rhythm that works for you. The more confident you are when reading or singing, the more fun you and the children will have.

- Get up and move! Demonstrate for the children the different ways to move their feet. Try it first with the children seated so they can focus on what you are saying. This supports play, background knowledge, and print motivation.
- Add voice inflection to emphasize the descriptive words. For example, for "stompity," make your voice deep and low; for "creepity," draw out the word "cre-e-e-e-pity"; for "clickity," make your voice higher and emphasize the click sound. This supports talk, vocabulary, and oral language.
- Encourage children to guess which animal is next in the book. Focus on the description given in the rhyme, and add additional information. For example, you might say, "Webbed orange feet! Who could it be?" Pause for a response. "The body is yellow, and this looks like blue water. It's a duck! Yes, it is a yellow, feathery duck with happy feet. A duck has webbed feet to help it swim." This supports talk, vocabulary, and background knowledge.
- Repeat the last page and insert the children's names. "Stompity! Stompity! Hear our feet! Who is dancing that stompity beat? Anna is dancing on stompity feet." This supports play and background knowledge.

Rhymes

Nursery rhymes are a childhood tradition. They have been passed down for generations. Using rhymes helps children develop early literacy skills, especially phonological awareness. The rhythm and rhyme of the words are fun for children, and this helps build an excitement about reading. Saying and singing nursery rhymes is a good way to help children hear the sounds of language, which will help them break words into parts when they are learning how to read.

Ada, Alma Flor, Isabel Campoy, and Alice Schertle. 2003. *¡Pío Peep! Traditional Spanish Nursery Rhymes*. New York: Rayo.
    This book is a collection of twenty-nine traditional Spanish nursery rhymes. The rhymes vary from poems to recite to rhymes that encourage engagement through movement. They are all reflective of Spanish and Latin American heritage, and each rhyme is accompanied by an English adaptation. If you do not speak Spanish, ask a parent who does to help you out.

Brown, Marc. 2013. *Marc Brown's Playtime Rhymes: A Treasury for Families to Learn and Play Together*. New York: Little Brown.

Do not let the title fool you—this book is not just meant for families. Teachers will find many uses for this collection of hand-and-finger rhymes. Brown includes illustrations with each line to show the movements that accompany the song or rhyme.

Calmenson, Stephanie. 2002. *Welcome, Baby! Baby Rhymes for Baby Times*. New York: HarperCollins.

The short poems, which are easy to chant or sing, chronicle the important activities of babies beginning at birth and moving through the first birthday. There are rhymes for just about all daily activities: diapering, going for a walk, naming body parts, doing what babies do, and making messes. After that first year, Calmenson has continued the rhyming fun with *Good for You! Toddler Rhymes for Toddler Times* that celebrates all the things toddlers can do.

dePaola, Tomie. 1997. *Tomie's Little Mother Goose*. New York: Putnam Juvenile.

dePaola's version of Mother Goose in this board book offers a variety of traditional rhymes. There is a good balance of rhymes that can be read with ones that have become more popular as songs. The rhymes do not include all the verses, which can get too long for young attention spans. Instead, the rhymes focus on the most familiar refrains.

Dyer, Jane. 1996. *Animal Crackers: A Delectable Collection of Pictures, Poems, and Lullabies for the Very Young*. New York: Little Brown.

The title says it all. Dyer has put together and beautifully illustrated a collection of familiar Mother Goose nursery rhymes interwoven with contemporary rhymes and poems. The book is divided into categories—ABC, 123, Shapes, Colors; Winter, Spring, Summer, Fall; Food, Food, and More Food; Animals, Animals; Nursery Rhymes; Playtime; and Lullaby and Good Night.

Foreman, Michael. 2002. *Playtime Rhymes*. Somerville, MA: Candlewick Press.

This collection of rhymes could be a staple in all early childhood classrooms. It includes more than seventy rhymes, many you may be familiar with but also some you may not have heard before. The illustrations are full of children, animals, and a few whimsical characters. An index in the back lets you easily find a particular rhyme. Also includes instructions or illustrations to include with each rhyme.

Hines, Anna Grossnickle. 2008. *1, 2, Buckle My Shoe*. Boston, MA: HMH Books for Young Readers.

What do you get when you combine a quilter with an author-illustrator? A beautifully illustrated rendition of the classic rhyme "1, 2, Buckle My Shoe." Though the rhyme may be familiar, the illustrations of quilted numbers take center stage in this hardcover book. If you are looking for a board-book version of this rhyme, try Salina Yoon's publication.

Kubler, Annie. 2003. *Ten Little Fingers*. Sydney, Aus.: Child's Play International.

This board book is part of Kubler's Nursery Time series. The familiar songs and rhymes have been specifically designed for babies. This book is a good introduction to well-known nursery rhymes and interactive text and includes musical notation, which aids in singing the rhymes. Other titles include *Head, Shoulders, Knees, and Toes*, and *This Little Piggy*. They are also available in Spanish/English versions.

Opie, Iona. 1996. *My Very First Mother Goose*. Somerville, MA: Candlewick Press.

> In combination with the work of Rosemary Wells, this nursery rhyme book, with its large, prominent illustrations and easy-to-see text, is beautiful. This book will work well for holding it with a child on your lap and for turning it outward for a small group of children to enjoy. *Here Comes Mother Goose* and *Humpty Dumpty and Other Rhymes* are part of this collection by Opie and Wells.

Scholastic. 2012. *Teddy Bear, Teddy Bear*. New York: Scholastic.

> Part of the Rookie Toddler series, this traditional rhyme involves movements that toddlers will enjoy: turn around, touch the ground, and touch the sky. The book includes tabbed pages that make it easy for little hands to turn them. Annie Kubler also has a board-book version of this rhyme in her Sign and Sing Along series.

Woodruff, Lisa, and Sarah Josepha Hale. 2011. *Mary Had a Little Lamb*. North Mankato, MN: The Child's World.

> The Favorite Mother Goose Rhymes series includes eighteen different titles. These hardcover books have sturdy pages for little hands that are ready to transition from board books to picture books. The book includes the rhyme and illustrations of children from diverse ethnicities.

Wright, Blanche Fisher. 2000. *My First Real Mother Goose*. New York: Scholastic.

> This board book includes fifteen nursery rhymes, including familiar ones such as "Baa, Baa, Black Sheep" as well as some that may not be as familiar such as "A Star." Wright has additional titles that include other rhymes: *The Real Mother Goose* and *Original Mother Goose*.

Yolen, Jane. 2013. *Wee Rhymes: Baby's First Poetry Book*. New York: Simon and Schuster.

> This collection of seventy-five rhymes covers all the activities of a baby's or toddler's day. Most of the poems are original, written by Yolen; however, there are a few familiar Mother Goose rhymes included throughout. Many of the rhymes encourage interactive play such as bouncing, clapping, and cuddling. Other activities are included such as identifying body parts and familiar objects. Great for language development!

How to Read It: *My Very First Mother Goose* by Iona Opie

- Add more information to nursery rhymes when you read or sing them. Ask questions about what is happening in the rhyme. Remember to pause and give children a chance to respond even if the response is a babble or a coo. For example, if you are reading "Little Boy Blue," you can ask, "Where is the boy sleeping?" Pause for a response. "Yes, he is sleeping under the haycock. (Note: Some versions of this rhyme use the word *haystack*.) Where do you sleep?" This activity supports talking, background knowledge, vocabulary development, and oral language.

- Nursery rhymes are full of new and unfamiliar words. The exposure is great for babies; as they get older, begin to explain the meanings of some of the words. As in the previous example, Opie uses the word *haycock* instead of *haystack*. Avoid substituting familiar words for any unfamiliar words; read what is there and then explain it. You can say, "*Haycock* is another word for *haystack*. Haycocks are small piles of hay, usually piled up in the shape of a cone." This supports talking, background knowledge, vocabulary development, and oral language.

- Bounce babies to the rhythm of rhymes, and move them to the actions described. For example, in "Jack Be Nimble," bounce to the words and when you get to "jump over the candlestick," pick the baby up and move him in an arc from one spot to another. Babies love it when the movements match the words. This supports play, vocabulary, and phonological awareness.

- Add children's names to nursery rhymes. "Jack be nimble, Jack be quick" can easily become "Sarah be nimble, Sarah be quick." This helps keep children's attention, and hearing their names acts as an anchor for them to listen to the next words. This supports talking and background knowledge.

- Use flannel-board stories with the nursery rhymes in the book. Either use store-bought pieces or make your own. Adding this literacy activity helps build more excitement about reading, supports play, and background knowledge.

- Since this book is large and has more than fifty rhymes in it, be prepared. Select the rhymes you want to read, sing, or use with flannel pieces. Mark the pages so you can easily move to the next rhyme. Reduce any waiting time for the children, and story times will go much smoother. This supports reading and background knowledge.

- Read some of the rhymes and sing others. Encourage children to join in with clapping or tapping to the rhythm. Singing nursery rhymes helps children get ready to read. Listening to rhymes helps them hear the smaller sounds in words and supports singing and phonological awareness.

- Add puppets to rhymes when possible. Using a sheep puppet to say or sing "Baa, Baa, Black Sheep" helps hold children's attention a little longer. Encourage children to play with the puppets also. You will soon hear toddlers repeating favorite rhymes with the puppets or stuffed animals in the class. This supports play, oral language, and phonological awareness.

Using Rhymes and Song Books with Infants

We use the term *story time* very loosely when talking about infants. Reading books with infants should be informal and should happen throughout the day. A story time using rhyming books and books you can sing in an infant classroom can look like the following.

- While you are rocking a baby—Sing a song or read a book that you can sing (even the one that you just sang) or sing or chant a fingerplay.
- While you are on the floor playing with a couple of children—Say a rhyme and include gestures, open a nursery rhyme book on the floor, read the book and talk about the illustrations, then sing another song.
- Gather a small group of children (who are interested) in the book area—Sing a song, read a book, and sing another song. As you know, their attention spans will be short. That's okay! Do not worry if some of these story times are only a minute long with the youngest children. Use your voice, make eye contact, and take your cue from what they are looking at.
- Even though these times may be very short due to a baby's attention span, it is important for you to be prepared and plan your book-sharing and literacy activities with infants. Use the story-time planning tools in Chapter 6. Your plan will not include as many items when you are planning for infants; however, having a plan will help keep you on track with what you want to accomplish with the children in your class. You can also use the sample story times that are provided; just modify them to fit the age and interest level of the children in your class.

Tips for Successful Story Times

- Pick times of day when the children are rested.
- Allow the children to pat and chew on the books.
- Encourage babies to touch the textures in books. You may need to help them by guiding their hands to the parts of the page.
- Repeat reading books that they show interest in.
- Use a high-pitched voice, and say words slowly and clearly to get a child's attention.
- Look at and talk about pictures.
- Allow children time to respond or imitate, even if they are not verbal yet.
- Choose books about things that children are familiar with.
- Point out words in books and in the environment.
- Lay a book on the floor, and face the baby while you are reading. The text will be upside down for you, but you can watch to see where baby is looking.
- Follow the baby's lead and interest, and talk about what she is looking at.

Sample Story Time for Older Toddlers and Twos

As children get older and their attention spans lengthen, you can begin to have a more "formal" story time with the class. It is okay if the children wander off; you can keep reading to the children who remain. The "wanderer" is most likely still listening and may rejoin the group. Initially your story time may only last about five minutes, but as toddlers grow you will be able to keep their attention for longer periods of time. Young children will be done with a book, song, or story time before you are. That doesn't mean you aren't doing it "right" or doing a good job. Expect that they will wander in and out of story time.

On the Farm

Song books and books with rhythm and rhyme give us endless opportunities to share books with infants and toddlers in joyful ways. Share the joy of reading and the lilt of language, and nurture developing early literacy skills throughout the day.

Choices of books, songs, rhymes, and fingerplays should be based on your preferences and those of the children in the class. This sample story time includes more stories and activities than young children will typically have the attention span for. Pick and choose your favorites. Always plan for more and adjust as needed. Watch the children's cues, and stop when needed to avoid frustration and behavior issues. Story times for infants and young toddlers should include more songs, chants, and fingerplays than books to keep their attention. Include in your newsletters, daily notes, or posts by the door information for parents about what you are reading and singing with the children.

- Use the same song to transition into your story time each time. This helps establish routine, and the children will learn very quickly that this cue means that books are next. Singing supports phonological awareness. Try the following song, or use any song you like.

  If You Want to Hear a Story
  If you want to hear a story, clap your hands. * (clap two times)
  If you want to hear a story, clap your hands. (clap two times)
  If you want to hear a story,
  If you want to hear a story,
  If you want to hear a story, clap your hands. (clap two times)
  *You can substitute "come sit down" for "clap your hands."

- Offer a description of the theme. Keep this very short and concise: "Today we are going to sing and read about farms and animals," or simply say, "It's story time!"

- Singing nursery rhymes helps children get ready to read. Listening to rhymes helps them hear the smaller sounds in words, which is phonological awareness. Sing a song related to the theme, such as "Mary Had a Little Lamb." Add a lamb puppet for more interest.

  Mary Had a Little Lamb
  (Note: All verses are included, but you may choose to sing only the first few.)
  Mary had a little lamb,
  Little lamb, little lamb,
  Mary had a little lamb,
  Its fleece was white as snow.
  And everywhere that Mary went,
  Mary went, Mary went,
  Everywhere that Mary went
  The lamb was sure to go.

It followed her to school one day
School one day, school one day
It followed her to school one day,
Which was against the rules.
It made the children laugh and play,
Laugh and play, laugh and play,
It made the children laugh and play
To see a lamb at school.
And so the teacher turned it out,
Turned it out, turned it out,
And so the teacher turned it out,
But still it lingered near.
And waited patiently about,
Patiently about, patiently about,
And waited patiently about
Til Mary did appear.
"Why does the lamb love Mary so?
Love Mary so? Love Mary so?"
"Why does the lamb love Mary so?"
The eager children cry.
"Why, Mary loves the lamb, you know.
Lamb you know, lamb you know."
"Why, Mary loves the lamb, you know,"
The teacher did reply.

- Read a book related to the theme, such as *Old MacDonald* by Rosemary Wells. As you read and sing this book, point to the picture of the animal when you get to the part of the story when the animal is named. This helps children make connections between pictures and words. You can also add a flannel story to this. Make each of the animals that you will sing about. When you get to the line, "And on his farm he had some _____." Put up the animal that is next. This helps develop print awareness and oral language.

- Sing a song related to the theme, such as "I Know a Little Pony." Bouncing to the beat of this action rhyme helps children hear and feel the rhythm of language.

I Know a Little Pony
I know a little pony. (bounce to the beat)
His name is Dapple Gray.
He lives down in the meadow
Not very far away.
He goes nimble, nimble, nimble (bounce double the beat for "nimble, nimble, nimble")
And trot, trot, trot. (bounce higher, but back to a slower beat)
And then stops and waits a bit. (stop bouncing)
Gallop, gallop, gallop, hey! (bounce for each gallop, and lift baby up on "hey!")

- Read a book related to the theme, such as *Moo, Baa, La La La!* by Sandra Boynton. Saying the sounds that animals make and encouraging children to make those sounds is the beginning of hearing the smaller sounds in words. This will help them as they decode or sound out words once they are learning how to read.

- Do a fingerplay, song, or rhyme, such as "These Are Baby's Fingers." Use movement and suit the actions to the words.

These Are Baby's Fingers

These are baby's fingers, (wiggle fingers)

And these are baby's toes. (wiggle toes)

This is baby's belly button. (circle finger on baby's tummy)

'Round and 'round it goes.

These are baby's eyes, (gently touch eyes)

And this is baby's nose. (touch nose)

This is baby's belly button (tickle tummy)

Right where (your name) *blows!* (buzz lips on baby's tummy)

- Just as with the opening song, sing the same closing song each time. Try the following song, or any song you like.

Story time is over now.

Story time is over now, over now, over now.

Story time is over now.

It's time to (fill in the blank with the next activity).

Chapter 4

Information Books

What's the Connection?

- Practice: Talk
- Components:
  - Background Knowledge
  - Vocabulary
  - Oral Language
  - Letter Knowledge
- Focus: Learning about My World

Babies have so much to learn, and they are ready! Their brains are wired to take in a lot of information. One of the best tools to use with little ones is exposing them to great books; however, exposure is not enough. We have to talk to them about what is in the books and add more information. There are many books available to teach children about their world. Research shows that the achievement gap in language development can be seen in children as young as eighteen months. A study by Anne Fernald published in *Developmental Science* showed that children from wealthier homes could identify words faster than children from low-income homes. Using information books, talking about the pictures in them, adding additional information as you read, and talking in full sentences rather than just labeling are all techniques that we must use with infants and toddlers to expose them to the many words that they need to hear.

There are many different kinds of information books. You may have heard the word *nonfiction*, which means factual books. In the public library, the nonfiction section includes poetry and folklore. For the purposes of this book and in early childhood education, the term *information book* refers to books that offer factual information about the child's world. These can range from very simple to more complex books that may have the following features:

- Pictures with labels
- Concepts such as alphabet, numbers, shapes, and colors
- Basic information about what is in a picture
- Explanations about the world and how it works

For infants, information books begin with simple, clear illustrations or photographs and only one or two words of text on a page. Typically, these books label the objects, items, or actions. For example, there might be a photograph of a dog and the word *dog* printed in bold text. Next, there might be a photograph of a cat with the word *cat* on the page. The story line might not be the most exciting, but what is happening when we read and talk about these books with an infant is more than exciting—it is amazing. Young children are learning that the word on the page is a representation of an object or action. Labeling books are a baby's introduction to learning that the words and sounds they hear are connected to what they see. Later when they begin to read, they will know what the word means without having a picture to accompany it.

Reading information books with clear, accurate pictures begins this process. Be sure to say more than just those one or two words that are on the page. Use the picture as a conversation starter.

The books and activities in this chapter are based on factual information. Books that label items and actions, describe things and places, or name emotions and body parts are all information books for infants and toddlers. You do not have to read information books from beginning to end. Instead, dip in and out of them, and spend as little or as much time on any given page as you or the child wants. Information books encourage vocabulary development. Labeling and describing objects teaches new words. Also, because the text is typically short we have the opportunity to have more conversation about what is in the book and add more information. Sometimes, when there is more text than the child will listen to, we can quickly read the text ourselves and then explain to the child what is happening in the picture. Use those interesting words! Do not dumb down the text, but use familiar words to explain the less familiar ones.

The Letter Knowledge Connection

Letter knowledge is knowing that letters are different from one another, that they can look different ways, and that letters represent sounds. Learning about the ABCs begins early, but children need to understand some basic concepts first. The very first step in learning about letters begins with learning about shapes. Researchers have found that children identify letters by their shapes. Other concepts, taught through reading books and the other early literacy practices that lead to letter knowledge, are knowing about opposites, similarities and differences, and colors. To help build letter knowledge, introduce simple puzzles. Exploring puzzles helps with size and shape recognition. All of these concepts come into play when determining the difference between one letter and another.

What to Look For

- Books that teach children information about the world around them
- Books with clear, accurate illustrations or photographs
- Books that explore cause and effect or comparison and contrast
- Topics may include concepts such as numbers, colors, or emotions
- Use books that have pictures of familiar and interesting things, people, and objects
- Uncluttered books that have few pictures on a page

Information books must be based on factual information. Typically, these books will have photographs, although there are good factual books that have illustrations. Include books that have familiar information for children, but also offer books that introduce new facts and words.

ALPHABET BOOKS

ABC books are a great way to introduce children to letters and their sounds. In this chapter, we have not focused on any specific alphabet books. The primary task when working with infants and toddlers is to build the foundation of concepts that leads to letter knowledge and understanding of the alphabet. There is nothing wrong with using ABC books with infants and toddlers; just remember that they are not developmentally ready to learn the alphabet. If you read ABC books, use them to expose children to letters and sounds. Keep it fun!

What You Can Do with Information Books

TIP

Children are naturally interested in exploring and making sense of their world. Information books help bring the outside world into the classroom.

Information books for infants and toddlers typically do not have much text. There is not always a story to tell. Instead, we have to provide more information. To get the most out of the experience and to keep it enjoyable for both you and the children, plan and be intentional about how you want to use the book. Books that offer factual information for children this age are, understandably, short. We have to talk to children about these books; talking with children is the key to developing their oral language. Looking at, for example, the wordless book *Who Are They?* by Tana Hoban with an infant may take at most twenty seconds to go from cover to cover. To make the experience much more meaningful, add information and language to the experience. Information books are closely tied to the practice of talking; however, they can be used in all of the practices that support children's growth and development. Providing information from books and in conversation is most directly connected to the early literacy components of vocabulary development, background knowledge, and letter knowledge.

Talk

Talking is the basis for all later literacy—early literacy and reading skills. Children need a strong basis in oral language and listening, speaking, and communication skills for later literacy. The way we talk with children makes a big difference in their early literacy development. Talking with children from the time they are born, making eye contact, watching their gestures and responses, and using words they are not familiar with are all ways to support early literacy.

Reading information books with children opens the door to a lot of communication. When we incorporate books that focus on factual information, we introduce many new words. Infants and toddlers need to hear these words. They may not understand all of them and that is okay. Exposure to words—lots of words—helps them build a large, strong vocabulary. Children who are spoken to frequently have larger vocabularies than children who are seldom spoken to—about five times as many words by the age of two. To build their vocabularies, we simply must talk!

Babies are most attentive to the first word you say after saying their names. Let's say there is a picture of a dog on a page. For the baby to really focus on the dog, you would say the child's name first and then the word as you point to the picture. For example, you could say, "Hadyn, dog," pointing to the picture. "See the dog? It's a white dog with black spots. When I was growing up, I had a black dog. I had to walk her in the park two times a day." It might feel more natural to say

"Hadyn, do you see the dog?" but then the first word after her name is *do*, not the main word we want the baby to focus on. Although it feels awkward at first, the more you practice talking this way, the easier it will become.

When we are talking with children, we can incorporate lots of information and different words into our conversations. Through talking we can help build their vocabularies, teach them new information, and begin laying the foundation of letter knowledge. For very young children, learning about letters begins with learning shapes, colors, and concepts such as *alike* and *different*. By integrating information into our conversations and book sharing with children, you can help them build skills that will support later learning to read. Describe things you see wherever you go: in the classroom, in the halls, outside on the playground. Talk about how the things you see are alike and different. Make comparisons of size, shape, color, and texture.

Describe pictures in books, and talk about how two pictures are alike and different. Filling our conversations with a lot of content or information and rich language is extremely important in infant and toddler classrooms. However, it is just as important to be intentional in how we talk with children. When you respond to a child's gestures, add words and description: "Carla, you're looking at the rattle on the floor and reaching for it. I think you want me to pick it up and hand it to you." Encourage a toddler's questions and curiosity about what you are reading. This not only teaches information when you answer their questions and explore what they are interested in, it also keeps them engaged. To help children learn new words, talk directly to them. Look at them while you are having a conversation. As you talk about what is in a picture, watch for a child's reaction. If you see the child reach, touch, or point to something on the page, repeat the word. Then add more information about the item or picture. Children will learn new information easier if we follow their lead and talk about what they are interested in. When reading one-on-one with a child, try facing the child. The book will be upside down to you, but you can then see what he is looking at on the page. Comment on that picture; describe it and ask questions. By following the child's lead, you are focusing on what he is showing interest in. Talk to babies in parentese when you are reading or during daily activities to get their attention. Babies will listen longer when you use a high-pitched voice, speak slowly and clearly, exaggerate sounds in words, and use short sentences.

Family Connection

Make word books with the children. (See page 74 for more information.) Show parents the word books you have made in class, and encourage them to make books at home with their children. Remind them to talk with their children, even if the children are not verbal yet, about the pictures and words that they put in the book. Remind them that it is important to give babies time to respond even if it is cooing or babbling. Give them suggestions for topics of books they can make. A good title includes the child's name, as it draws her attention to the word that follows: *Daniel's Day, Carla's Toys, TJ's Pets, Maurice's Family.*

Write

Just as books can have different purposes, writing has different purposes. When children are older and become writers themselves, they will use writing in many ways. To prepare them for the many purposes of writing, we can begin very early with activities that will build the foundation they will need to be successful in school.

When you read a book with a child, point to a word that is on the page as you label a picture. By doing so, children begin to see that those words are related to the picture on the page, which is print awareness. Let children see you write, and explain what you are writing. For example, you might say, "I have to write down what time you had your bottle so your mommy will know how much you ate today." Encourage toddlers to scribble, write, and draw themselves.

Family Connection

Give parents a list of developmentally appropriate art activities for their children. Display the children's art projects in the classroom so parents can see what children at this developmental age are capable of. Encourage families to provide time at home for scribbling and coloring. Let them know that these activities will help their children get ready to write.

Read

The simplest information books have very few words—essentially they are labelling books. There may be a picture of an object and the name of the object, or a photograph of a cat and the word *cat*. These types of books are very appropriate to read with infants and toddlers. They are the basis of developing the concept that the word represents the object. When reading this type of book, read the word then add more information. Talk in complete sentences; this adds richness to their vocabulary and helps children build on their background knowledge. Talk about the picture and expand on what is there. For example, if there is a picture of an apple, you can say that apples grow on trees, even if there is not a picture of a tree in the book. You can say that we eat many things made of apples such as applesauce and apple pie. Even though children will understand the words for objects and things they can see more easily, we still need to use all kinds of words with them: words for actions, concepts, feelings, and ideas. Exposure to words is the first step to understanding them later, developing a strong vocabulary, and learning about the world, which is part of background knowledge.

In addition to adding more information when reading a book, have the real objects available. This is another way that children begin to learn that words represent things. For example, if a book has pictures of toys, such as blocks, rattles, dolls, and so on, show them the real things. Make connections for the child between the real object and what is in the book. If you are reading a book that shows a bib, you can say, "Here is a picture of a bib. The one in the book is purple with a butterfly on it. You have a bib on, too. Yours is blue with white stripes." When you make these types of connections and speak to children in complete sentences, you are filling their day with a lot of rich language, which will help build a strong vocabulary.

Read books to babies that have real photographs of faces. Children show a preference for faces more than objects. Increase children's print motivation by offering books that children are interested in.

When you are reading a book with pictures or illustrations, use different words for the same picture. Read the word on the page and then offer additional words or synonyms. You might say, "Cup. That is a cup. Some people call it a mug or a drink." Exposing children to different words for the same object lays the groundwork for developing a large vocabulary. Begin using information books with infants that are about things they know—cup, bottle, baby, and so on. As they get a little older, read books about things they may not see every day—deer, train, dump truck, and so on. Even in short, simple books, there may be unusual or rare words. Read the uncommon words, and avoid substituting an easier, more familiar word. You can give the familiar word as a synonym to help explain. Books have about three times more unusual words than we use when we talk with our children. Read them again and again. You may talk about the pictures a little differently each time. That's fine!

Have fun with these books. Young children are just beginning to build relationships with books and reading. If you are having fun, they will too. Books that are focused on factual information do not have to be boring; they can be just as fun as silly rhyming books. When you keep it light and have fun with the books, pictures, and language, you are helping to develop a love of reading, which is part the background knowledge, particularly print motivation.

There is information all around us. Read labels, signs, and logos. Make sure that your classroom has labels throughout, and remember to read them so the children can start making connections that they mean something.

Family Connection

Encourage families to use information books with their infants or toddlers. (See sample letters in Chapter 7). Explain the importance of teaching the names of people, places, and things. Give parents lists of words you have introduced to the children through the books you have read or the activities you have done during the day.

Sing

Some songs can help with remembering sequences in nature. For example, you can make up a song to the tune of "Here We Go 'Round the Mulberry Bush": This is the way we plant the seed, water the seed, and so on. Singing is a fun way to learn information as well as develop phonological awareness and learn about the world around us. You can sing just about any book for infants and toddlers. The text in informational books is short, so you can add a little rhythm to your voice and make it a song. This will grab their attention because it sounds different from regular reading. When you want to reinforce ideas, themes, and concepts, sing a song or rhyme after reading a related book. For example, after reading a book about farm animals, sing "Old MacDonald Had a Farm." This type of activity or sequence of activities incorporates quite a few skills: phonological awareness, background knowledge, and vocabulary.

Family Connection

Give families the words to songs you have sung, along with the information the songs support, especially if you make up songs to fit particular topics.

Play

When we are playing with children, there are many opportunities to exchange and teach information. The way we talk about what we are playing with and how we describe objects helps children learn about them. Play sorting games during play time, cleanup, or daily activities. For example, when you are putting toys back into bins during cleanup, you can say, "The wooden blocks go in here. They are square and hard. The cloth blocks go in this bin. They are soft and have different colors. This one is red, and this one is blue." Sorting items and learning about their colors, shapes, and textures are fundamental components of building letter knowledge.

Playing games with infants can foster their development in many ways. Play tracking games with them. This helps babies develop their focusing skills, which they will need to look at pictures in books and to become aware of print. When they are very young, keep the objects close, about eight to fourteen inches in front of them. As they improve their tracking ability, move objects a little farther away. You can also play How Big—this works well on the changing table. While the baby is lying on the table, ask, "How big is the baby?" or "How big is (child's name)?" Raise the baby's arms over her head and say, "Sooooo big!" Remember to watch for signs of distress.

If the baby does not seem to enjoy this, change to another activity such as singing to calm her. Although at first you will be moving her arms, the baby will quickly begin responding on her own. These are just a few examples of how playing can help babies learn about their world, develop vocabulary, have fun, and get ready to read. Use your imagination, and be creative as you play with the children in your classroom.

Even very young children will have preferences about what they like and what they might not be as interested in. As you observe the children in your class, pay attention to these preferences. Print motivation is the early literacy skill that focuses on a child's enjoyment of books and reading. One way to encourage this is to offer choices. Allow children to pick books that you will read, and offer choices during play time.

Even with information books, you can play. Incorporate puppets, stuffed animals, and other props, and use them to reinforce ideas or concepts in a book. If a book is about toys that babies play with, gather those toys together and play with them while you read.

Family Connection

Urge parents to play with their children in front of a mirror. Let them know that children use their names as an anchor; they pay more attention to the word that immediately follows their name. You can give families a list of suggested comments and questions to use with their children:

- "Look at your smiling face. You look very happy today."
- "Sienna, how big are you?" Raise her arms over her head. "You are soooo big!"
- "Marcus. Shirt. You have on a red shirt." Point to and touch his shirt. "Your shirt is soft."
- "What are these?" Pause for a response. "Sam's toes. These are your cute little toes. How many do you have? Let's count. One, two, three, four, five!"

Don't have an information book handy or the titles we have suggested? You can add additional information to any experience, book, or activity. Just talk!

- Narrate what you are doing or what the children are doing.
- Tell them the steps in a process.
- Read labels and signs aloud.
- Talk to babies in parentese: use a higher voice and say words slowly and clearly.
- Talk about and describe feelings.
- When you are reading other types of books, add information and use descriptive language.
- Use a lot of concept words—shapes, sizes, opposites, and similarities.
- Use a lot of prepositions and words that describe spatial relationships.
- Put words to how a child might be feeling. You might say, "I can see you are frustrated because the tower of blocks keeps falling down."

Talk about everything, even if the children do not understand everything you are saying or if they cannot answer your questions. Talk to children in encouraging ways; this will help them succeed later. Offer choices: "Which toy do you want to play with, the cars or the blocks?" Explain reasons: "Your jacket will keep you warm. It's cold outside." Describe what will happen during the day. Allow five to ten seconds after you speak, and then give a response yourself. Ask questions such as the following:

- What happened?
- What are you doing?
- What are you going to do next?
- What might happen?

Make word books with the children. They can be made out of small photo albums or folders with paper or sheet-protector sleeves inserted. Ask families to send in photographs of their child, family members, pets, or favorite toys. Use the books with each child; they will recognize the familiar people and objects. This offers opportunities to ask questions and describe the pictures. If you cannot get photos from home, make books out of pictures from magazines.

Information Books about Babies

Babies love to look at pictures of faces and babies. Many of the books in this list include real photographs of babies from many cultures and ethnic backgrounds. Reading books about where babies go, how they get there, and what they feel helps them build knowledge about the world around them.

DK Publishing. 2009. *Baby Faces Peekaboo!* New York: Dorling Kindersley.

This lift-the-flap book addresses four sets of feelings: happy and smiley, sad and grumpy, silly and funny, and tired and sleepy.

Emberley, Rebecca. 2005. *My Garden/Mi Jardín*. New York: Little Brown.

Emberley's series of eight Spanish and English board books covers topics that babies and toddlers are familiar with. The set includes *My Food/Mi Comida*, *My Colors/Mis Colores*, *My Clothes/Mi Ropa*, *My Toys/Mis Juguetes*, *My Animals/Mis Animales*, *My Numbers/Mis Numeros*, and *My Shapes/Mis Formas*. In all the books, images are set on a stark white background for high contrast. They are simple; only one or two words in each language are on each page. Even though the text may be sparse, remember to add more information. Talk about the objects and pictures, expand on what is in the book, and ask questions.

Foord, Jo. 1995. *Good Morning, Baby!* New York: Dorling Kindersley.

This series of soft-covered board books, which includes *Good Night, Baby!*, *All about Baby*, and *Baby and Friends*, is perfect for little hands. They are full of colorful photographs of babies and toddlers doing familiar activities with familiar objects. These titles are also available in Spanish. There is limited text, so they are short to read but offer many opportunities to add more information, descriptions, and stories.

Geller, Amy. 2013. *My First Words Outside*. Cambridge, MA: Starbright.

There is a lot to learn about the great outdoors! This labeling book with photographs includes many words from interesting places—the garden, park, beach, farm, and forest.

Global Fund for Children. 2007. *Global Babies*. Watertown, MA: Charlesbridge.

This series, which includes *Global Baby Girls* and *American Babies*, has short simple text and striking photographs of children from many countries and ethnicities. They address universal concepts, such as being loved and changing the world, and they expose children to people from different cultures.

Greenstein, Elaine. 2004. *One Little Seed*. New York: Viking Juvenile.

The garden and what happens there is a whole new world for children. This beautifully illustrated book captures in very simple text the process of a seed growing into a plant.

Grossman, Rena. 2009. *Carry Me*. Cambridge, MA: Starbright.

Part of the Babies Everywhere Board Book series, this book shows babies being carried in many ways. The book has a simple rhyming text and photographs of babies from around the world. They are wrapped in blankets, in baskets and backpacks, and held in a parent's arms.

Martin, Bill, Jr., and John Archambault. 1998. *Here Are My Hands*. New York: Henry Holt.

The content is factual but it is illustrated as opposed to having real photographs. The rhyming text is interesting to young children and offers information about body parts and what they can do.

Miller, Margaret. 2009. *What's on My Head?* New York: Little Simon.

The real photographs of babies in this book show little ones with familiar objects on their heads. The pages alternate between appropriate headwear, such as hats and bows, and silly items, such as a frog and a rubber duck.

Page, Stefan. 2014. *We're Going to the Farmers Market*. San Francisco, CA: Chronicle.

This book is filled with bold colors and shapes, not to mention a lot of information about going to the farmer's market, selecting fruits and vegetables, then cooking them.

Pinkney, Andrea, and Brian Pinkney. 1997. *Pretty Brown Face*. San Diego, CA: Red Wagon.

Unlike many of the other books in this list, *Pretty Brown Face* is illustrated. It includes a short sentence on each two-page spread that identifies a body part then gives a description of it.

Scholastic. 2013. *Ears, Eyes, Nose*. New York: Scholastic.

Children love to learn about their bodies. Part of the Rookie Toddler series, this book has photographs that show a variety of toddlers touching familiar body parts. The book includes ears, eyes, nose, fingers, mouth, and toes.

Scholastic. 2013. *What Happens Next? Seed to Plant*. New York: Scholastic.

One of the titles in the Rookie Toddler series, this book takes place in the garden. Photographs of toddlers show them planting, caring for, and then eating tomatoes. Children can begin developing sequencing skills with this type of book. Talk to them about what happens first, next, and last in the story.

Slier, Debby. 2012. *Cradle Me*. Cambridge, MA: Star Bright.

Slier has collected beautiful photographs of Native American babies in cradle boards. Each page includes a picture and one verb describing what the baby is doing: yawning, thinking, peeking, and so on. There is a blank under each word to fill in a word in another language. You could also use this as a prompt to fill in a synonym or more description.

Slier, Debby. 2013. *Loving Me*. Cambridge, MA: Star Bright.

Similar to her title *Cradle Me*, Slier has captured beautiful photographs of Native American babies. In this simple book, babies and young children are shown with family members who love them.

Star Bright Books. 2011. *My Face Book*. New York: Star Bright.

The cute babies in this book will be very interesting to other babies. The photographs of faces are paired with a word for the emotion. As you read, watch as babies begin to mimic the expressions they see in the pictures.

Verdick, Elizabeth, and Marjorie Lisovskis. 2013. *Reach*. Minneapolis, MN: Free Spirit.

Part of the Happy Healthy Baby series, other titles include *Eat, Move, Cuddle*, and *Play*. This series focuses on early developmental milestones. The black-and-white photographs of babies are paired with an opposite page that has a bright background and illustrations. Babies are shown doing what babies do: reaching, grasping, eating, crawling, and squirming. The books offer suggestions and tips for parents and caregivers.

Yoon, Salina. 2011. *At the Park*. New York: Feiwel and Friends.

Yoon's series of four simple concept books, which includes *At the Farm, In the Ocean*, and *At the Beach*, uses die cuts and foil to keep baby interested. These first-word board books include descriptive words to identify familiar objects, places, and items.

How to Read It: *Eat* by Elizabeth Verdick and Marjorie Lisovskis

The books in this series focus on early developmental milestones. Babies are shown doing what babies do: reaching, grasping, eating, crawling, and squirming.

- Read the book and emphasize the rhyme and rhythm. Although this is an information book, it has a rhyming text that you can read or even give a little lilt to your voice and almost sing. This supports reading, singing, background knowledge, and phonological awareness.
- Take advantage of the close-up photographs. Point out the facial features and body parts shown. Point to the body part in the pictures, then point to the baby's. If the baby is showing interest, go beyond the basics and point out and label teeth, tongue, eyebrows, and lips. This supports talking, background knowledge, and vocabulary development.
- Imitate the actions or activities in the books. Imitating activities is early learning for pretend play later on. This supports play, talking, and background knowledge.

- Add more conversation to the book. You probably know information about the babies in your class, such as some of their favorite foods. When reading *Eat*, you can add to the sentence, "Banana, cereal, milk, or toast . . . What does baby like the most?" You can ask, "Sam, what do you like to eat the most?" Pause and give time for a response, even if it is just cooing or batting at the page. "That's right! You like applesauce. Apples are sweet and good. I can tell you like them because you smack your lips when you eat them." This supports talking, background knowledge, and vocabulary development.

Information Books: Objects

Reading books about items and objects that children are familiar with helps them understand the facts about them. Young children will develop preferences; some will like books about trucks, while others will like books about toys. Find what children like, and stock your shelves with books on those topics.

Blake, Michel. 2007. *Baby's Day*. Somerville, MA: Candlewick Press.

> The books in this series were made for infants and toddlers. They feature simple contrasting photographs of babies with one object at a time and only one word that labels items such as teether, chair, and bib. They are designed with slightly graduated pages, which help children in learning to turn pages. This was originally a series with quite a few titles; however, only *Baby's Day* and *Out to Play* are currently in print. Check your local library for additional titles.

DK Publishing. 2010. *Tractor*. New York: Dorling Kindersley.

> Part of the Baby Touch and Feel series, this book has padded covers for little hands to grab and carry. The series includes other titles such as, *Puppies and Kittens*, *Colors and Shapes*, *Mealtime*, *First Words*, and *Animals*. These books offer experiences that adults and children will want to repeat again and again. Each book offers information about items related to the topic of the title. *Tractor* includes descriptive words along with transportation sounds. Not only will children learn factual information about tractors and other hard-working vehicles, but they can also play with the sounds they make: "brrm! brrm! brrm!" and "chug! chug! chug! chug!"

Emberley, Rebecca. 2002. *My Food/Mi Comida*. New York: Little Brown.

> Emberley's set of eight Spanish and English board books covers topics that babies and toddlers are familiar with. The set includes *My Colors/Mis Colores*, *My Clothes/Mi Ropa*, *My Toys/Mis Juguetes*, *My Garden/Mi Jardín*, *My Animals/Mis Animales*, *My Numbers/ Mis Numeros*, and *My Shapes/Mis Formas*. In all the books, images are set on a stark white background for high contrast, and only one or two words in each language are on each page. Talk about the objects and pictures, and expand on what is in the book and ask questions.

Hill, Eric. 1997. *Spot's Favorite Words*. New York: Warne.

Eric Hill's beloved Spot introduces infants and toddlers to names and labels of familiar objects. This book is full of colorful illustrations that grab the attention and focus on objects in baby's world.

Hines, Anna Grossnickle. 2010. *I Am a Backhoe*. Berkeley, CA: Tricycle.

This informational book also encourages imitative play. As you read about the boy who is pretending to be each type of machine, you and the children can pretend along with him. This is a sturdy-page hardcover book that not only teaches about different types of machinery, it also has a rhythmic text and sounds that are great to play with: "swooooshhh," "beep," and "smash."

Hoban, Tana. 1994. *What Is That?* New York: Greenwillow.

High-contrast pictures and illustrations in books are great for babies. This board book features one familiar object per page. The pictures are white on a black background. The title is a prompt—by asking, "What is that?" on each page, you and baby can label the items. Remember to give infants time to respond even if they are not verbal yet. When you give the answer, use sentences and avoid just labeling.

Lovitt, Chip. 2011. *My Giant Tractor*. White Plains, NY: Reader's Digest.

Additional titles in this series include *My Red Fire Truck* and *My Big Dump Truck*. These fact-filled sturdy board books have handles that make them easy for toddlers to carry around. They include lots of information about the uses of each vehicle and the jobs they can perform. Children are also encouraged to look for colors, shapes, and different objects throughout the book.

Miura, Taro. 2006. *Tools*. San Francisco, CA: Chronicle.

This sturdy-page hardcover book covers the many tools that are needed for various professions. Familiar tools and professions are included, such as wrench and mechanic, and hammer and carpenter. However, the book also introduces children to tools and professions that you might not typically talk about, such as bent-nose tweezers and watchmaker.

Page, Liza. 2009. *Trucks*. New York: Innovative Kids.

The E-Z Page Turners series was developed with the help of child-development experts. The books are designed with graduated pages that help little ones learn how to turn them. Real photographs of the trucks are combined with illustrations. The simple text gives the name of each truck. Other titles in the series include *Shapes*, *Colors*, *Counting*, *Opposites*, and *Mommies and Babies*.

Rockwell, Anne. 2014. *Trucks*. London: Walker.

Even though the characters are not factual—cats do not really drive trucks—the information about all kinds of working vehicles is. The text is short but very informative and covers many different trucks, from fire trucks to garbage trucks to campers.

Scholastic. 2013. *What Rhymes?* New York: Scholastic.

Part of the Rookie Toddler series, this book focuses on rhyming sounds. A single photograph on each page is paired with a rhyming item: frog/dog, spoon/balloon, mouse/house. Children can begin developing their ability to hear rhyming words with this type of book. Encourage them to think of other words that rhyme.

How to Read It: *Trucks* by Anne Rockwell

This book can be used with a variety of ages. For younger ones, you may use more labeling; the names of all the trucks are given. With older children who are ready for more information, there is a short statement that describes what each type of truck is used for.

● With children who love trucks, you will be able to read this book from beginning to end. Repeated readings of books are very beneficial for children. If this book (or any other) is a favorite, read it over and over. This supports reading and background knowledge.

● If children are familiar with the information in the book, focus on different pieces of the information during repeated readings. For example, during one reading you can focus on the characteristics of the trucks. You can say, "This delivery truck is pink and has a picture of a flower on the side. That flower looks like a rose. This truck has four wheels. You can see two of them, and there are two on the other side." On another reading you can focus on the type of work the truck performs. You can say, "Tow trucks tow away cars. If a car breaks down or has a flat tire, a tow truck can take it to the garage for repairs." This supports talking, vocabulary development, and background knowledge.

● Ask children questions. If they do not know the answer, you can help by giving them a choice, making it an either/or question. You can ask, "Which truck keeps things cold?" Pause. "Is it the tow truck or the refrigerator truck?" Pause for an answer. If they still do not respond even after waiting five to ten seconds, say the answer. Especially for babies, you will say the question, pause, and then say the answer. This supports talking and background knowledge.

● Point out similarities and differences in the trucks. Describe and talk about size, function, and number of wheels. This supports talking, background knowledge, and vocabulary development.

● Build on what is familiar to children and add more information. If there are particular trucks that you know they are familiar with, talk about that with them. For example, you can say, "We see the garbage truck here in the parking lot every Tuesday. The truck comes and takes away all of the garbage from our school. Does the garbage truck come by your house?" Pause for a response. "Once the truck picks up all of the trash, it takes it to the landfill. That is a big place outside of town where all the trash goes." This supports talking, vocabulary development, and background knowledge.

● When you are playing with trucks in the classroom, say the name of the truck and provide additional information about the type of truck it is and the work it does. You can say, "Michael, please push the dump truck over here. The dump truck can carry heavy loads then dump them out." This supports play, talking, vocabulary development, and background knowledge.

● Imitate trucks while you are playing. You can use *I Am a Backhoe* by Anna Grossnickle Hines to help with this activity or let the children use their imaginations. Remember to add sound effects—trucks are not quiet. This supports play, phonological awareness, and background knowledge.

Information Books: Concepts

Information books help teach basic concepts that are the foundation for a child's later learning success. Information books can support learning not only when it comes time to learn to read but also in relation to math, science, critical-thinking skills, emotions, and relationships.

Bang, Molly. 1996. *Ten, Nine, Eight*. New York: Greenwillow.

> Although this book is a countdown to bedtime, it can be incorporated into read-aloud times in the classroom. Books about routines help reinforce what children know, their background knowledge. This book also offers the opportunity to count and guess: "Where is the black cat?" Look for him throughout the book.

DK Publishing. 2005. *Los Colores del Bebé/Baby Colors*. New York: Dorling Kindersley.

> This book and *123 Bebé/Baby 123* are Spanish and English books about colors and shapes. They are fun to read together and have simple text and colorful images that encourage conversation, labeling, and exploring two languages.

Emberley, Rebecca. 2000. *My Shapes/Mis Formas*. New York: Little Brown.

> Emberley's set of eight Spanish and English board books covers topics that babies and toddlers are familiar with. The set includes *My Food/Mi Comida, My Colors/Mis Colores, My Clothes/Mi Ropa, My Toys/Mis Juguetes, My Garden/Mi Jardín, My Animals/Mis Animales*, and *My Numbers/Mis Numeros*. In all the books, images are set on a stark white background for high contrast. They are simple with only one or two words in each language on each page. Even though the text may be sparse, remember to add more information. Talk about the objects and pictures, and expand on what is in the book and ask questions.

Grossman, Rena. 2009. *Eating the Rainbow*. Cambridge, MA: Star Bright.

> This title is part of the Babies Everywhere series. The photographs embrace children from many diverse backgrounds.

Hoban, Tana. 1993. *White on Black*. New York: Greenwillow.

> Distinct, clear images set against a black or white background help young developing eyes focus. These simple wordless books, including *Black on White* and *Black and White*, offer many opportunities for conversation. Talk about the pictures and relate them to what the baby knows. *Black and White* offers both styles of contrast in an accordion-style book. Just reverse it and you have the opposite contrast. This format is great for laying open on the floor or placing by a changing table.

Katz, Karen. 2003. *Counting Kisses*. New York: Little Brown.

> An information book can look like a storybook with colorful, cartoonlike illustrations. The content just needs to be factual. This cuddly kissing book counts down from ten to one and includes descriptive words that help build concepts related to feelings as well as numbers.

Page, Liza. 2008. *Counting*. New York: Innovative Kids.

> The E-Z Page Turners series was developed with the help of child-development experts. The books are designed with graduated pages that help little ones learn how to turn them. Real photographs of the trucks are combined with illustrations. The simple text gives the name of

each truck. Other titles in the series include *Shapes*, *Colors*, *Opposites*, *Trucks*, and *Mommies and Babies*.

Pictall, Chez. 2007. *Spots and Dots*. Lanham, MD: Cooper Square.

Part of the Art Baby series, this book and *Hearts and Stars* are designed for our youngest readers. The high-contrast images are stimulating; they help the brain and eyesight to develop as babies focus on the distinct images.

Priddy, Roger. 2004. *Bright Baby Colors*. London: Priddy Books.

Part of the Bright Baby series, which includes *Bright Baby First Words*, *Bright Baby Animals*, and *Bright Baby Trucks*, these information books help support vocabulary development with their simple format. They have simple clear photographs with one descriptive or labeling word per page. The series is also available in bilingual formats.

Scholastic. 2013. *Red Apple, Green Pear: A Book of Colors*. New York: Scholastic.

Another title in the Rookie Toddler series, this one focuses on identifying colors. A single photograph on each page has a short simple sentence that names the fruit and its color. The last page gives toddlers the opportunity to match fruits with their colors.

How to Read It: *My Shapes/Mis Formas* by Rebecca Emberley

The books in this series have simple, high-contrast images with only one or two words in each language on each page.

- Remember to add more information as you talk about the objects and pictures, and expand on what is in the book and ask questions. This supports talking, vocabulary development, and background knowledge.

- Read bilingual books even if you do not have children in your class that speak a language other than English. Exposing children to other languages and pronunciations of words will help expand their vocabulary. If you do not know how to pronounce a word, ask a parent for help. This supports talking, vocabulary development, and background knowledge.

- This book easily lends itself to use with a flannel-board story and game. Make flannel shapes (a great way to use up scraps of felt), then make the additional pieces to form the objects. For example, cut a circle and some small dots and a skinny piece for the string. Put the shape up first, label it in both languages, then add the dots and "string." Label the balloon in both languages. Depending on the children's ability and attention span, add more information. Allow older toddlers to help put the pieces on the flannel board. This supports play, vocabulary development, background knowledge, and letter knowledge.

- Continue to point to and label shapes and objects from the book throughout the day. Keep the book handy to make references to. For example, if there is a toy truck in the classroom, you can say, "Diane, truck. That is a truck, *el camión*. We saw a truck in the book." Show the picture and point to the truck. "This shape on the back is a triangle, *el triángulo*. It is a red triangle. Can you say *red triangle*?" Pause and wait for a response, even if it is babbling. This supports talking, vocabulary, background knowledge, and letter knowledge.

- Encourage children to make shapes with their hands and bodies. Shapes are the foundation of letter knowledge. Demonstrate for the children, and help them as needed. Make a circle with your fingers or a triangle with your arms. This supports play and letter knowledge.
- Point out colors and shapes all through the day. Talk about the color of the children's clothing, hair, shoes, and so on. This supports talking, letter knowledge, and vocabulary.

Information Books: Animals

Animals are part of our world, and young children love learning about them. There are a lot of areas to cover in this topic, including the names of animals, the different types, the habitats, the animals' sounds, and their behavior. Begin with what the children know and are familiar with, and move on to animals that they may have never seen or heard of before.

Appleby, Alex. 2013. *I See a Butterfly*. New York: Gareth Stevens.

> This title is part of the In My Backyard series. Other animals included in the series are chipmunks, ladybugs, frogs, squirrels, and birds. These hardcover books introduce children to familiar animals and offer basic facts about them and their lives. These books are also available in Spanish/English versions.

DK Publishing. 2009. *Baby: Baa Baa!* New York: Dorling Kindersley.

> This title is part of the Baby Chunky Board Books series. Other titles include *Baby: Night Night!*, *Baby: Colors!*, *Baby: Woof, Woof!*, and *Baby: Hide and Seek!* In *Baby: Baa Baa!* the colorful pages are paired with photographs of cute farm animals. Descriptive words throughout provide information about animals found on the farm.

Hnatov, Catherine. 2010. *Hip, Hop*. Cambridge, MA: Star Bright.

> This is a high-contrast book that is good for infants. The information is short and simple, and the black-and-white images show cute animals that young children are familiar with. Short sentences offer information about what each animal says or does.

Hoban, Tana. 1994. *Who Are They?* New York: Greenwillow.

> This wordless, high-contrast book has black images of adult and baby animals set against white backgrounds. The number of babies increases from one lamb to five ducklings. This book offers opportunity to add more information about the animals and teach the names of the babies.

National Geographic Kids. 2014. *Baby Animals*. Washington, DC: National Geographic Society.

> Part of the Look and Learn series, National Geographic introduces children to baby animals with their trademark photography. Animal facts as well as a matching game are included in this beautiful book.

Priddy, Roger. 2002. *Happy Baby Animals*. New York: Priddy Books.

> The Happy Baby series includes informational books on many topics, including words, colors, the alphabet, and things that go. *Happy Baby Animals* has clear pictures of animals and includes the habitats where they live.

Rizzi, Kathleen. 2012. *Who Lives Here?* Cambridge, MA: Star Bright.

> These books are available in many languages: Portuguese/English, Spanish/English, and Arabic/English. One title in the series focuses on pets, and another focuses on forest animals. The pictures give choices of the five animals included in the book with a picture of a home. Lift the flap to see which animal lives there.

Sami. 2006. *Woof-Woof.* Maplewood, NJ: Blue Apple.

> This title is part of the Flip-a-Face series. Other titles include *Who is Sleeping?, Who is Awake?, Baby Animals, Big Little, Colors, Play!,* and *Furry Friends: Same and Different.* Cutouts in *Woof-Woof* change one animal face to another, ending with baby's face.

Schindel, John. 2010. *Busy Birdies.* Berkeley, CA: Tricycle.

> This series includes board books with beautiful pictures of animals doing what animals do. The titles include *Busy Barnyard, Busy Chickens, Busy Piggies, Busy Doggies,* and *Busy Elephants.* Each vivid photograph is paired with simple rhyming text that describes the animal's actions. This book introduces verbs that you may not typically use on a daily basis.

How to Read It: *Busy Birdies* by John Schindel

- If you have feathers in your room, let the children feel the feathers—be careful with little ones who still take everything to their mouths. Children are learning through all of their senses. Provide opportunities for them to feel different textures and shapes. Talk with them about what feels the same and what feels different. This helps them later when they try to make out the shapes of letters and try to figure out what is the same and different among them. This supports play, talking, letter knowledge, and background knowledge.

- Add texture books that are related to the animals in the books. This provides tactile experiences to connect with the names of the animals. This supports talking, background knowledge, and letter knowledge.

- Add information as you read this book. You may have to do a little research if you are not familiar with bird species and their habits. Even though the book does not give the bird names, you can tell the children what types of birds they are. For example, you can say, "That is a hummingbird. They are very tiny and can hover, which means they can move their wings but stay in one spot. Not all birds can do that." This supports talking and background knowledge.

- Sing songs about birds. There are lots to choose from: "Five Little Ducks," "Two Little Blackbirds," or "Two Little Dickie Birds." This supports singing and phonological awareness.

- Throughout the day, refer to verbs that are used in the book. When you see a child doing one of the activities, talk about it. For example, you can say, "Latonya, you are stretching. That is what the bird was doing in the book. See." Show the picture if the book is handy. "This white bird with pink wings is stretching too." This supports talking and background knowledge.

Information Story Time with Infants

A story time using information books in an infant classroom can look like the following:

- While you are rocking a baby, sing a song that has hand movements, read a book that labels objects, talk about the objects using descriptive words, and add more information, then sing another song.
- While you are on the floor playing with a couple of children, say a rhyme and include gestures, open an information book on the floor, have real items that are included in the book, encourage children to play with the items, read the book and talk about the different objects, then sing another song.
- Gather a small group of interested children in the book area. Sing a song, read a book, then sing another song.

Their attention spans will be short. Do not worry if some of these story times are only a minute long with the youngest children. Use your voice, make eye contact, and take your cue from what they are looking at. Even though these times may be very short, it is important for you to be prepared and plan your book-sharing and literacy activities with infants. Use the story-time planning tools in Chapter 6. Your plan will not include as many items when you are planning for infants; however, having a plan will help keep you on track with what you want to accomplish with the children in your class. You can also use the sample story times provided; just modify them to fit the age and interest level of the children in your class.

Tips for Successful Story Times

- Pick times of the day when children are rested.
- Allow children to pat and chew on books.
- Encourage babies to touch the textures in books. You may need to help them by guiding their hands to the parts of the page.
- Repeat reading books that they show interest in.
- Use a high-pitched voice and say words slowly and clearly to get a child's attention.
- Look at and talk about pictures.
- Allow children time to respond or imitate, even if they are not verbal yet.
- Choose books about things that children are familiar with.
- Point out words in books and in the environment.
- Lay a book on the floor, and face the baby while you are reading. The text will be upside down for you, but you can watch to see where the baby is looking.
- Follow the baby's lead and interest, and talk about what she is looking at.

Interactive Story Time with Older Toddlers and Twos

As children get older and their attention spans lengthen, you can begin to have a more formal story time with the class. If the children wander off, you can keep reading to the children who remain. The wanderers are most likely still listening and may rejoin the group. Initially your story time may only last about five minutes, but as toddlers grow you will be able to keep their attention for longer periods of time. Young children will be done with a book, song, or story time before you are. Expect that they will wander in and out of story time.

All about Me!

This is a sample story time to highlight information books. For a well-rounded, enjoyable story time, you will need to combine a variety of books and styles of reading. Choices of books, songs, rhymes, and fingerplays should be based on your preferences and those of the children in the class. Remember to consider the children's ages, likes and dislikes, attention spans, and developmental levels. This sample includes more stories and activities than young children will typically have the attention span for. Pick and choose your favorites. Always plan for more and adjust as needed. Watch their cues and stop when needed to avoid frustration and behavior issues. Story times for infants and toddlers should include more songs, chants, and fingerplays than books in order to keep their attention. Include in your newsletters, daily notes, or posts by the door information for parents about what you are reading and singing with the children.

- Use the same song to transition into your story time each time. Singing helps support phonological awareness. Using the same song each time helps establish routine; the children will learn very quickly that this cue means that books are next. Try the following song, or any song that you like.

  If You Want to Hear a Story
  If you want to hear a story, clap your hands. * (clap two times)
  If you want to hear a story, clap your hands. (clap two times)
  If you want to hear a story,
  If you want to hear a story,
  If you want to hear a story, clap your hands. (clap two times)
  *You can substitute "come sit down" for "clap your hands."

> **TIP**
>
> These books typically have little text. Be prepared and plan ahead so you can add more information, props, or actions to the books. Offer a good balance of different types of books to match the interest level and abilities of your particular group.

- Offer a description of the theme. Keep this very short and concise: "Today we're going to read about how wonderful you are," or simply say, "It's story time!" This supports print motivation and print awareness.
- Sing a song related to the theme. Singing is fun! Do not worry if you do not have perfect pitch. In songs, each syllable has a different note, and the children hear words broken into parts. This phonological awareness helps them when they have to sound out words. You can write the lyrics on a whiteboard or sheet of paper and point to them as you sing. This visual aid helps develop print awareness as the children make the connection between the written words and the lyrics. Demonstrate the actions on a baby doll or stuffed animal. You will soon see children imitating the actions with the dolls in dramatic play.

  This Is Baby

  This is baby ready for a nap. (hold doll in your arms)

  Lay baby down in a loving lap. (lay doll gently in your lap)

  Cover baby up, so he won't peep. (cover doll with blanket)

  Rock baby till he's fast asleep. (rock doll in your arms)

- Read a book related to the theme, such as *Here Are My Hands* by Bill Martin, Jr., and John Archambault. This book comes in different formats: board book, hardcover, and big book. Using a big book during story time allows all the children to see the pictures easily. Choose the format that works best for your group. If you choose to use it with very young children, they may not be able to focus on the pictures as easily as older ones; however, they will still love hearing the sound of your voice. Encourage children to touch and identify the body parts that are in the book.
- Sing another song or chant related to the theme, such as the following:

  Head, Shoulders, Knees, and Toes

  Head, shoulders, knees, and toes, (touch head, shoulders, knees, and toes)

  Knees and toes. (touch knees and toes)

  Head, shoulders, knees, and toes, (touch head, shoulders, knees, and toes)

  Knees and toes. (touch knees and toes)

  And eyes and ears and mouth and nose. (touch eyes, ears, mouth, and nose)

  Head, shoulders, knees, and toes, (touch head, shoulders, knees, and toes)

  Knees and toes. (touch knees and toes)

  This song is easy to make a flannel cutout for. Just find a pattern or draw a child's body; coloring books are a great resource for patterns. As you sing the song, point to the parts of the body. If you do not have a flannel cutout, use your body or touch the parts of the children.
- Read a book related to the theme, such as *My Face Book* by Star Bright Books. The cute babies in this book will be very interesting to other babies. Each photograph of a face is paired with one word for the emotion. As you read, watch as babies begin to mimic the expressions they see in the pictures. Demonstrate the expressions for children and ask questions. You can say, for example, "I wonder why this baby is crying." This supports vocabulary development, reading, and talking.

- Sing a song related to the theme, such as the following:

  If You're Happy and You Know It

  If you're happy and you know it, clap your hands. (clap, clap)

  If you're happy and you know it, clap your hands. (clap clap)

  If you're happy and you know it, and you really want to show it,

  If you're happy and you know it, clap your hands. (clap clap)

  If you're sad and you know it, say, "Boo-hoo." (say "boo-hoo" and rub eyes)

  If you're sad and you know it, say, "Boo-hoo." (say "boo-hoo" and rub eyes)

  If you're sad and you know it, and you really want to show it,

  If you're sad and you know it, say, "Boo-hoo." (say "boo-hoo" and rub eyes)

  This is a good follow-up to any book about emotions. Include the emotions from *My Face Book*. Avoid making the song too long so you do not lose the children's interest.

- Do another fingerplay, such as the following:

  These Are Baby's Fingers

  These are baby's fingers, (wiggle fingers)

  And these are baby's toes. (wiggle toes)

  This is baby's belly button. (circle finger on baby's tummy)

  'Round and 'round it goes.

  These are baby's eyes, (gently touch eyes)

  And this is baby's nose. (touch nose)

  This is baby's belly button (tickle tummy)

  Right where (your name) *blows!* (buzz lips on baby's tummy)

- Just as with an opening song, singing the same closing song at the end of each story time signals to the children that story time is over. This song offers a smooth transition into the next activity. Sing the following song or any song you like.

  Story time is over now.

  Story time is over now, over now, over now.

  Story time is over now.

  It's time to (fill in the blank with the next activity).

Using information books with young children opens up worlds for them and for us as well. From labeling pictures—information in its simplest form—to adding further information, talking about concepts, and learning about the world, we capitalize on children's curiosity. It is the love of learning that will motivate children to learn through reading.

Chapter 5

Storybooks

What's the Connection?

- Practice: Read
- Components:
    - Background Knowledge
    - Print Awareness
    - Phonological Awareness
    - Vocabulary
- Focus:
    - Cognitive Development
    - Sequencing
    - Narrative Skills

What makes a story a story? How are these books different from others? A story, whether you are reading it in a book or telling it, has some very important parts:

- Characters: they may be imaginary, animals, or people
- Plot: events happen; there is a beginning, a middle, and an end
- Purpose: teaching a lesson or providing entertainment

Reading and telling stories help children develop *narrative skills*, the ability to describe things and to talk about events and tell stories. These are skills they will need when it is time to learn how to read. Although narrative skills have a lot to do with oral-language development, reading stories helps build a strong foundation for children. Good narrative skills help them develop comprehension and help them understand the structure of story, which is part of background knowledge. Many stories include repeated phrases, such as "Not by the hair of my chinny-chin-chin," or patterns, such as three bears and three chairs or three pigs, which help children recognize these motifs later on. Stories help children learn about experiences, places, and things that they may not be exposed to in their everyday lives. For example, in *Froggy Gets Dressed* by Jonathan London or *The Snowy Day* by Ezra Jack Keats, children learn about snow. If they live in an area that does not get much snow in the winter, that may be a new experience for them. Stories also help children learn sequences: what happens first, next, and last? Storybooks help children learn how to handle books and how books work. In English, we read from front to back and left to right. Storybooks follow this format.

Reading stories with young children sometimes does not look like reading at all. There is—and should be—a lot of back-and-forth conversation going on. Keep in mind that a child's response may be through gestures, batting at a page, kicking his legs, or gazing at you while you talk and read. The more interaction there is between you and the child while reading, the more you are helping build important skills.

TIP

Read books that you love. If you are having fun, infants and toddlers will pick up on that, and they will have fun, too.

There may even be times that you are not reading any of the words on the page, but you can and should talk about the pictures. Children need to hear lots of words. Reading and telling stories is a critical piece of the puzzle in providing them with all of the words they need to hear. Children's books have about thirty-one "rare" words per thousand words. That is three times more than is typically heard in conversation and 25 percent more than we hear on television shows. The more of these rare words children know, the easier it will be when it comes time for school. This is just one more great reason to read books with children.

What to Look For

- Stories about familiar topics and subjects
- Clear, accurate illustrations; avoid cluttered pictures
- Simple story lines and plots
- Stories with repeated words or phrases
- Stories that rhyme
- Stories with interesting sounds, animals, transportation, or silly words

There are so many storybooks out there. Sometimes it can be overwhelming trying to decide which ones to pick. An infant who is not mobile will listen to long stories while you rock and cuddle her. More mobile children who have a lot to explore may only sit for a couple of minutes to hear a story. Offer a mixture of types of books to capture all of the children's interests and abilities.

What You Can Do with Storybooks and Storytelling

Reading stories is an integral part of how children learn the skills they will need to be successful readers later. Storybooks are great for reading and for retelling stories. There are so many things you can do with storybooks:

- Read them, of course!
- Retell the story without the book.
- Use props such as flannel-board pieces, a story glove, or a story apron as you read or retell the story.
- Talk about the pictures in the story.
- Predict what might happen next by saying something such as, "Hmm, I wonder what might happen next."
- Repeat reading favorite stories.

> **TIP**
>
> Read with expression! Give characters different voices. Change the tone and sound of your voice while you are reading to emphasize what is happening.

Read

Reading aloud to children is the single most important activity to help children become successful readers. The way we read with children and the types of books we read really matter. When we read stories to children, there are lots of techniques and strategies we can use that help children build early literacy skills. Reading the words in the book is important because sometimes books use interesting words we do not use in regular conversation with young children. It is also important to talk about what is happening in the pictures of the book, to help children relate what is happening to their own experiences. This helps later with comprehension. By occasionally pointing to the pictures and words in the book and reading the title, we help them develop print awareness, understand how books work, and learn that print has meaning. Encouraging children to repeat the words you have pointed to builds vocabulary.

Helping children enjoy books goes a long way when they are later learning to read in school. Children who have had enjoyable experiences around books and reading are more likely to stick with learning to read even if it is difficult for them. Encourage a child's active participation in book reading. When she wants to turn a page, say, "Oh, time to turn the page." Encourage the child to repeat what you say. In books with a repeated phrase, say the phrase, then encourage the children to repeat it with you. When you are reading a story, you can say, "Let's start at the beginning, with the front cover." As you finish, close the book and say, "The end. All finished!" This helps them learn story structure. As you are reading stories, emphasize repeated letter sounds. Do this for exposure to the sounds and to build letter knowledge, but keep it enjoyable—there is no need to force it. Repetition is important! Repeat reading stories to children. Research shows that repeated reading helps children comprehend the story better and helps develop vocabulary.

As you are reading to infants and toddlers be aware of their behaviors and what captures their attention. Very young children who have limited oral language will use gestures to communicate with you. Put words to a child's gestures. When a baby is chewing on a book, you can say, "Oh, that book looks good. Let's read it together. Encourage babies to talk, babble, or coo as you read books. While reading, watch what the baby is looking at on the page, what captures his attention or interests him, and talk about it.

Family Connection

Let parents know that you read every day in the classroom, and explain how important reading books with children—even very young babies—is. Use the print-awareness sample letter in Chapter 7 to explain the importance of reading. List books that you have read on the children's daily sheet, or post a list of titles on the door or in another visible spot in the classroom. As you observe children and learn what their favorite books are, tell their parents. Encourage families to take their children to the local library where they can find a lot of different books.

Play

There are a variety of ways to incorporate play into reading stories. Try adding props such as flannel-board pieces and puppets. These types of activities not only engage children in fun ways, but they also help children's comprehension of the story and its content. Even without props, we can play with a story. Act out what the characters are doing, and encourage children to imitate what activities are happening in the story. Modeling or demonstrating an action is more effective than just telling the children to make a smiley face or jump up and down. To make it fun, show them that you are having fun and show exactly what you are asking them to do.

While children are playing, put words to their actions and describe what is happening. Be careful to not disrupt their play as you do this. Think of it as narrating their actions. You can say, "Jackson, you are building a very tall tower. You have stacked up so many blocks." When we describe what they are doing, it helps build their background knowledge by putting an explanation to what is happening. This also brings in more vocabulary to their day. Be sure to add new words or descriptive words to your narrations.

In addition to narrating and describing while children are playing, ask questions and incorporate sounds. Ask open-ended questions during play to encourage conversation, such as, "Jimmy is holding the doll and rocking her. Sara, how do you think Jimmy is feeling?" Give children plenty of time to formulate their answer. If they do not know the answer, give them a choice of two options and see if they repeat one of your choices. Or give them a response and encourage them to repeat it: "Jimmy is feeling happy and showing love to the baby doll."

Incorporate sounds from books into your play with children. Make car sounds such as "Vrrooomm," animal sounds such as "Meow," and silly sounds such as "Zip, zap, zup!" Engaging purposefully in children's play in these ways can provide many opportunities to emphasize skills such as background knowledge, phonological awareness, and vocabulary.

Family Connection

Share with families all the ways they can play with books, language, and rhymes. Let them know that by allowing their child to play with books, they help them learn to have fun. Having fun, enjoying, and being comfortable with books helps build print motivation, which helps children get ready for reading success.

Write

Writing skills are just beginning to emerge in very young children. To help them get ready for actually writing later on, there are activities we can incorporate every day to help support building those skills. Play action rhymes with babies and toddlers to help their fine-motor development. Encourage them to scribble and draw; scribbling is a very important prewriting skill. Ask children to tell you about their "pictures." Avoid asking, "What is it?" Instead, just encourage them to tell you anything about the scribble, such as "blue" or "dog." And remember that their scribbles may not be about anything in particular at all. Write down stories that children tell you, and encourage them to add pictures to their stories. These types of activities not only help build a foundation for writing, they also support the idea that print has meaning.

Family Connection

When you write down children's stories, give them to the parents. Let families know that reading and writing go together. Suggest to parents that they encourage their children to talk about the scribbles and that they avoid asking, "What is it?" Instead, they can say something such as, "Tell me about your drawing." The process of scribbling and drawing is so much more important than the end product. Encourage parents to allow their young children to scribble and draw. Give parents a list of appropriate writing and art materials. Even older infants can begin scribbling, with supervision of course. Remind parents that a child's scribbles don't have to mean anything or be "about" anything in particular. Scribbling is a first step to later writing.

Sing

Learning about stories, how they work or their structure, what happens next or the sequence, and what they are about are important skills for young children. Singing can reinforce these concepts. Sing songs and rhymes that include sounds from stories you read. If you read a book about farm animals, then sing a song with animal sounds in it. This reinforces the information that is in the story and adds to a child's background knowledge. Sing songs and use fingerplays that count up or down. With very young children, you can reduce the number; for example, you can sing about three green and speckled frogs instead of five. These types of songs help children understand sequences.

Family Connection

Give parents a list of songs that have sequences in them. Be sure to include the lyrics and actions. For young children, these will typically be counting up or down songs. Later, the children will be ready for more complex songs that are cumulative, such as "There Was an Old Lady Who Swallowed a Fly."

Talk

Encourage children to talk as you read books. Sometimes it is appropriate to read a book from beginning to end without stopping for conversation, and sometimes it is helpful to stop and talk about something interesting in the book. Use both styles. With young children, if you are going to read without stopping, use very short books. Talk about a picture in the book, and pause and wait for babies to babble back to you. Encourage babies to babble or talk, and repeat what a baby says. Add your own words, and praise them when they imitate you. Babbling is actually the beginning of their oral-language development; it is a baby's vocabulary.

Other ways to help build not only vocabulary but also their knowledge of the world around them are to tell stories, ask lots of questions, and describe children's actions. Ask questions about the book or a page in the book, then wait five to ten seconds for a response. If the child does not know the answer, you can give the answer and ask them to repeat it. Use either/or questions to help children get the correct answer. For example, you can ask, "Did the gorilla unlock the cages or go to bed?" Expand on their answers: "Yes, he unlocked the cages, and all of the animals followed the zookeeper home." Tell stories to the children. They do not have to be long elaborate ones; you can tell short stories throughout the day about a variety of topics and experiences. Put words to children's actions. For example, when a child is smiling, comment, "Oh, you are so happy!" As a baby moves her hands and feet, ask, "What are you so excited about?" When a baby turns his head away or arches his back, say, "Time for a break." When a toddler points to the shelf, ask, "What would you like to play with?"

Family Connection

Encourage parents to tell their children stories. Even infants like to hear the rhythm of a parent's voice when they are reading or telling a story.

Questions are great tools for building vocabulary and oral language. Asking questions helps build vocabulary and background knowledge and narrative skills in particular. When asking questions about a picture in a book, avoid asking, "Where is the _____?" This type of question allows children to just point to the object in the picture instead of answering with words. *What* questions are the easiest to answer. This is a very good place to start; however, to expand vocabulary and comprehension, you have to go much further with questioning and conversation. Simply asking, "What is that?" will most often elicit only a one-word response. When you ask a *what* question, always add more information. Repeat the child's answer, and then give more detail. Encourage the child to repeat what you have said. For example, point to a picture in a book and ask, "What's that?" Allow time for the child to babble or talk. Say what the picture is, label it, and describe the picture using full sentences. Give the child a chance to say something again. Keep the back-and-forth exchange of information going as long as the child is interested.

When asking children questions, try to keep them open-ended, such as the following examples. Offer choices for answers, always give children plenty of time to respond.

- What do you see on this page?
- Look at the boy's face. How do you think he is feeling?
- What is the girl in the picture doing?
- Is she riding a tricycle or running after a dog?
- What do you think is happening here?

Help children have success at answering questions. It is okay to use fill-in-the-blank questions and to give children clues if they are trying but cannot quite come up with the answer or word they are looking for. The purpose of asking questions is to encourage verbal responses and conversation, not to quiz children to see if they know the "right" answer. Keep it light, and help them when they need it.

Don't have a storybook handy or the titles we've suggested? You can make any book into a story, even one that only has one word labeling an item on a page. You just have to add the information. You can also make any event into a story. For teachers who are not comfortable talking a lot, especially with very young children who do not talk back to continue the conversation, this can be a bit uncomfortable or awkward. That's okay. With practice, you will become more comfortable.

Narrate what you are doing during daily routines: go through the sequence of changing a diaper, talk about what happens next when washing hands, or tell children what will happen next. Tell children stories. They do not have to be long, elaborate ones. Tell them about what happened as you were driving to work or what you are going to do after school that day. Encourage children to tell you stories about what they are doing or something they are familiar with. Ask them about their pets, what they had for breakfast that morning, or what their favorite toy is and why.

Episodic and Simple Stories

Episodic books have a simple story line and a very loose plot. Essentially, the experiences that the character has are different on each page. Skipping a page would not change the understanding of the story. These types of storybooks are a good introduction to more complex story lines that children will be ready for soon.

Bedford, David. 2008. *Tractor, Tractor!* Melbourne, Aus.: Little Hare.

Hardworking tractors make learning about opposites fun. Each two-page spread shows two different tractors with rhyming descriptions. Some are described by color, others by characteristics such as old, new, fast, and slow. When you are talking about the pictures in the book, remember to point out and talk about similarities, too.

Campbell, Rod. 2007. *Dear Zoo*. New York: Little Simon.

This lift-the-flap book will keep children guessing about which animal the zoo has sent. For younger children, use the picture clues to help them guess. You can see the giraffe's head above the door or the lion through the bars. For older children, use the clues in the text: the giraffe is described as too tall, the lion as too fierce. The book has different vocabulary words to introduce such as *fierce, grumpy, scary, naughty, jumpy,* and *perfect*. Explain these words, give synonyms, and demonstrate them for the children.

Carle, Eric. 2005. *Does a Kangaroo Have a Mother, Too?* New York: HarperCollins.

Repetition is the name of the game in this book. This story is included in the episodic section because each page does not necessarily connect to the next; you can skip an animal and the story line will not be changed, just shortened. The question-and-answer style of the text offers opportunities for children to answer. Until they are familiar with the information, pause for five to ten seconds, and then continue reading to supply the answer. Factual information is included in the back of the book that provides the names of all the babies, parents, and animals.

Fleming, Denise. 1996. *Lunch*. New York: Square Fish.

This hungry little mouse eats a lot of yummy, colorful vegetables and fruits. The story is short and simple but fun for children as they see how much he eats and how messy this little mouse is. The book works well to emphasize colors as well as the names of fruits and vegetables.

Fox, Mem. 1997. *Time for Bed*. New York: Red Wagon.

A singsong lullaby book, this is a good choice for snuggling or getting a tired infant or toddler settled for rest time. Each page has two sentences that rhyme but do not necessarily connect to the next page. If you skip pages in this book, it will not change the rhythm or story that you are telling.

Guarino, Deborah. 1997. *Is Your Mama a Llama?* New York: Scholastic.

Rhymes, repetition, and riddles make this a fun book to read. The book introduces six baby animals. Encourage older children to guess what the animal is, using the pictures as clues. You can also encourage older children to ask the repeated question, "Is your mama a llama?" If the book gets too long for some, you can skip one of the animals to shorten it.

Hill, Eric. 1985. *Spot Goes to the Beach*. New York: Putnam Juvenile.

Hill's beloved character Spot is having fun getting ready for and spending the day at the beach. The flaps in this book add to the fun of reading the story. Use them to make this an interactive book. They are good prompts for questions such as, "What do you think he is doing?" or comments such as, "I wonder what is under there."

Keats, Ezra Jack. 1976. *The Snowy Day*. New York: Puffin.

The main character, Peter, has different experiences in the snow. He makes tracks in the snow, knocks snow from a tree, builds a snowman, and makes snow angels. Each experience is essentially a separate event.

Wood, Audrey. 1999. *Silly Sally*. New York: Red Wagon.

Sally heads to town in a very silly way, and she meets some silly friends as she goes. The rhyme and repetition of the text will quickly engage young children who will want to experiment with the different ways of moving. Expect giggles while reading this book and children who will want to get up and try walking backward or even upside down. This book is available in a variety of formats: big book, hardcover, board book, and oversized board book.

How to Read It: *Silly Sally* by Audrey Wood

Select the appropriate format of this book depending on the way you are going to read it. If you are reading to a group of children, a big book might be a good choice. For reading one on one or to just a couple of children, a board book or hardcover version may work better. Keep this favorite in board-book format on the shelf for children to select on their own.

- Practice this book before reading it for the first time to the children. Practice reading it with rhythm. This supports reading and phonological awareness.
- Use your voice when you are reading this book. Emphasize the silly lines. This will draw children's attention to those sentences, which supports print awareness and reading.
- If children enjoy this book, reread it. Repetition helps children learn new words and understand the story. You can change your focus or emphasis with repeated readings. For example, if you have emphasized the silly sentences during one reading, emphasize the rhyming words another time. This supports reading, phonological awareness, and background knowledge. As children become familiar with the story, use the pictures as clues to what is coming next. Each two-page spread shows the next animal and even shows Neddy Buttercup. He is very small at the beginning of the book. This helps children begin to predict and supports talking and background knowledge.
- Play with this book. Encourage children to try to walk like Sally. They can try to sing or dance while they are walking. This supports play, background knowledge, and print motivation.
- Have explanations or synonyms ready to explain unfamiliar words. Children most likely do not know what a loon is, or a jig, or even the word *tune*. This supports talking and vocabulary development.
- Encourage children to retell this story. They may not get the order correct, but they may remember all the animals and Neddy Buttercup. This supports talking and background knowledge.
- Use flannel-board pieces as you read this story or retell it. Allow children to help put the pieces on the board. Actively involving children in telling the story helps them learn and remember what you have read to them and keeps them engaged. This supports reading, play, background knowledge, and print motivation.

Stories about Solving Problems and Working Things Out

Stories help children learn about their world and how to solve problems. These stories have simple story lines, and each one of the characters learns how to overcome a problem or accomplish something. You can read them to all ages; however, older toddlers will have a better understanding of the full meaning of the stories.

Burningham, John. 1990. *Mr. Gumpy's Outing*. New York: Square Fish.

What happens when there are too many in the boat and everyone is not on his best behavior? They fall in, of course! This story has a cumulative style in which the animals and their behaviors are repeated. It may be a bit long for young toddlers, but older ones will have a good laugh when the animals misbehave and fall in the water.

Cohen, Miriam. 2000. *Mine! A Backpack Baby Story*. Cambridge, MA: Star Bright.

This is a simple story of a child on an outing with his dad. The child shows each of his items, ranging from a fire engine to a book to juice. His dilemma? Deciding if he wants to share. This book is also good for naming and labeling items.

Dewdney, Anna. 2005. *Llama, Llama, Red Pajama*. New York: Viking.

Bedtime is a routine that children are familiar with, and most can relate to the difficulty Baby Llama has with it. The repetition and rhyming make this fun to read and listen to. Encourage children to chime in on "llama llama red pajama." The book uses words children may not be familiar with: *alone, fret, whimpers, moan, hollers,* and *wailing* are just a few.

Numeroff, Laura. 1999. *The Best Mouse Cookie*. New York: HarperFestival.

A simple story that introduces children to the funny mouse from *If You Give a Mouse a Cookie*, this story is much shorter than Numeroff's picture books and is just the right length for babies and toddlers. Mouse has a grand time baking but falls asleep and burns the cookies. Not to worry: throw them out and start over. Problem solved!

Stiegemeyer, Julie. 2006. *Cheep! Cheep!* New York: Bloomsbury USA Childrens.

The chicks have to find out what that noise is! With minimal rhyming text and interesting pictures, this book tells the story of a new chick joining the family. Since the text is short, add more information to the story line to explain what is happening.

Thompson, Lauren. 2011. *Leap Back Home to Me*. New York: Margaret McElderry.

Little frog is learning how to brave the world on his own, with his mother close by, of course. This book has a nice rhyming text and fun words such as *plip* that are good for playing with sounds.

Wells, Rosemary. 2003. *Ruby's Tea for Two*. New York: Viking Juvenile.

Ruby and Max are two favorite characters for children. Max is again up to mischief at the tea party his sister, Ruby, is having with her friend. Max is the server, but he has a problem: He wants to join the tea party. By putting spiders on the cupcakes, he solves his problem by scaring Ruby and her friend. He can then have tea and cake.

How to Read It: *Mr. Gumpy's Outing* by John Burningham

This book has words that children may not be familiar with, such as *squabble, tease, muck, bleating,* and *trample.* Be prepared with explanations for those words. Do not worry about explaining each one of them during the first reading; the children will lose interest.

- Prepare the children before reading the book. You can give an overview of what is going to happen. You can say, "In this book there are a lot of animals. We are going to read about a goat, a calf, chickens, sheep, a pig, a dog, a cat, and a rabbit." Then encourage children to make the sounds of all these animals. This supports talking, phonological awareness, and background knowledge.

- Animal sounds are not included in this book, but you can add them. This will keep children interested, especially infants. Encourage them to make the animal sounds while you are reading to keep them involved and help them play with sounds. This supports talking, phonological awareness, and print motivation.

- After repeated readings, some children may be able to associate an animal with its action. This is a great time for fill-in-the-blank questions or statements to allow children to help tell the story. You can say, "And the goat (pause)." If they do not get the answer, that is okay. After a five-to-ten-second pause, you can fill in the blank. If they give the incorrect answer, remain positive. You can say, for example, "The cat is the one who chased the rabbit. The goat kicked." This supports talking, background knowledge, vocabulary development, and oral language.

- You can also use either/or questions with this book. You can ask, "Did the goat kick or flap?" Answering either/or questions may be easier for children who do not have the oral language to answer open-ended questions with confidence. This supports talking, background knowledge, and vocabulary development.

- Extend this book throughout the day. Provide materials and help children pretend to ride on their own boat. What animals will they bring? What happens if the boat gets too full? This supports play and background knowledge.

- The story ends with all of the characters having a tea party. Provide items for the children to have their own tea party. Make connections for the children. You can say, "In the book we read Mr. Gumpy has tea with his friends. We have a teapot and teacups just like in the story." When children reenact what happens in a book, it helps them remember the story. This supports play and background knowledge.

Stories about Routines and Daily Activities

Routines are important to young children. They help them learn what to expect and how to respond to the world around them. Routines also help children learn to make decisions and appropriate choices. Stories that cover predictable routines and daily activities are appropriate for infants and toddlers as they can relate to the content and story line.

Barton, Byron. 2003. *My Car*. New York: Greenwillow.

> Sam drives his car from day until night and through sun and rain. Byron's simple story of Sam and his car will entice toddlers with lots of information about cars, their parts, and taking care of cars.

Brown, Margaret Wise. 1947. *Goodnight Moon*. New York: HarperCollins.

> A classic book read by many teachers, parents, and children. Children quickly learn the rhythm and rhyme of this book as they associate with the familiar routine of going to bed. Because this is such a familiar book to children, add more to the story by focusing on the pictures. Talk with them about what is in the pictures, describe objects, and ask questions as you read this book.

Carlstrom, Nancy. 1996. *Jesse Bear, What Will You Wear?* New York: Aladdin.

> Jesse moves through his day that is filled with dancing in the morning, eating a healthy lunch, and bathing at night. Reading the entire book may be a little long for young toddlers; however, the rhyming text and quick rhythm of the book will hold children's attention. The story covers an entire day and includes favorite toddler activity: picking out their own clothes! Jesse even chooses to wear a chair!

Cohen, Miriam. 2014. *Daddy's Busy Day*. Cambridge, MA: Star Bright.

> From morning to night, this toddler and Daddy have a very busy day while Mommy is at work. This sweet story of a young child and dad follows them through familiar activities from breakfast to house work to a trip to the park.

Dewdney, Anna. 2012. *Llama, Llama, Nighty-Night*. New York: Viking Juvenile.

> Reading stories and cuddling with Mama help Baby Llama get ready for bed. Dewdney's easy rhythm and rhyme address a familiar routine that children can identify with. This title, as well as others in this series, is in board-book format. The story is a bit shorter than the hard-cover versions—perfect for the younger set!

Galvin, Laura. 2011. *Baby Pig: Time to Play*. Washington, DC: Smithsonian.

> Baby Pig has a full day of adventures. This board book with photographs of piglets offers a lot of information about what pigs do. *Baby Pig* goes from morning to night and shows this cute animal playing with friends, rolling in dirt, and climbing rocks.

Lewis, Kevin. 2001. *Chugga-Chugga Choo-Choo*. New York: Disney Hyperion.

> This hardworking train begins with waking up in the morning and ends tucked in bed ready for sleep. The rhythmic and rhyming text also includes train sounds that help children play with words. Make sure to read every "Whoooo! Whoooo!" It helps the story flow and

continues the rhyme throughout. You can also point to the words *whoooo whoooo* to show the difference in how the text is written and adjust your voice to call attention to the difference.

London, Johnathan. 1994. *Froggy Gets Dressed*. New York: Puffin.

In Froggy's excitement to get out in the newly fallen snow, he quickly dresses but forgets some important items. This book includes fun sounds as clothes, boots, and coats go on.

Wells, Rosemary. 2004. *Max's Breakfast*. New York: Viking Juvenile.

Max is still up to his mischievous antics in this book about breakfast routines. Wells's series of Max books covers many routines and events that are familiar to young children. This series has seven other titles: *Max's Bath, Max's Bedtime, Max's Birthday, Max's First Word, Max's New Suit, Max's Ride,* and *Max's Toys.*

How to Read It: *Chugga-Chugga Choo-Choo* by Kevin Lewis

This rhyming picture book brings a toy train to life as the child plays before bedtime. The bright illustrations and rhythmic text keep the attention of young children. The train's freight of different toys and the repeated phrases, "Chugga-chugga choo-choo" and "Whoooooooo! Whoooooooo!" offer plenty of opportunities for children to talk about what is happening in the pictures and to retell parts of the story.

- If you are using the board book, allow the baby to turn the pages even if he can just bat them. If he is interested in chewing on the book, you can offer another book to chew on or a toy to mouth. This supports reading and print awareness.

- Point to the picture on the cover and say, "(Child's name), train. Look at the picture on the cover. It's a picture of a train—a train engine!" Allow time for the child to babble back. Using the child's name first helps draw his attention to the word or picture you are talking about. This supports talking and vocabulary development.

- Talk about what is on the title page of a book. Draw children's attention to the pictures, and add more information. You can ask, "Jason, what does a train say?" Pause for a few seconds. Allow time for the baby to babble back to you. Then say, "Chugga-chugga choo-choo! Yes! Chugga-chugga choo-choo. This train engine is black, and it has red wheels." This supports talking, background knowledge, and vocabulary.

- As you turn pages, you can talk about what is being loaded on the train. You can say, "Jada, duck," as you point to the duck. "Look, they are loading a toy duck on the train." If the child is looking at the picture and not turning the page, you can read the text. Then say, "Let's see who is watching the train go by. Oh, look, Jada, rabbit—a rabbit with big ears. The rabbit is watching the train go by." This supports talking and vocabulary development.

- Look at babies and encourage them to look at you as you say, "Whooooo! Whooooo! The train whistle says, 'Whoooooo! Whoooooo!'" Wait several seconds and see if babies will try to imitate you. They may imitate your lip position even if they do not say the words. This supports talking and vocabulary development.

- Some of the pages show a lot of different toys. Watch to see what children are looking at on the page. Talk about what they are looking at—that is what they are interested in. This supports talking and print motivation.
- When you finish reading the book, say, "The end." This helps children learn story structure, supports reading, and supports print awareness.
- After finishing the book, you can ask, "Shall we start again?" Watch for cues that the children are interested in more reading. If so, read it again. If they want to turn the pages quickly, then "the end" will come quickly, too. That's okay. This supports reading and print motivation.
- Encourage children to say, "Chugga-chugga choo-choo," and "Whooooo! Whooooo!" throughout the book. Actively engaging the children will keep their interest, and these words help them play with sounds. This supports talking, phonological awareness, and print motivation.

Stories with Repetition

Stories with repeating lines help children grasp the meaning of the story. They also gain a sense of accomplishment as they learn the lines and can repeat them when you are reading aloud. Encourage children to repeat lines in a story. When they participate in reading the story instead of just listening, they will comprehend much more.

Begin Smart Books. 2008. *All Gone!* New York: Begin Smart.

> This is a thick, foam-filled page book. The thick pages are easy for little hands to turn. Children will be familiar with the foods that become "all gone" in this story about cereal, juice, cookies, and other favorite treats.

Isadora, Rachel. 2008. *Uh-Oh!* Boston, MA: Houghton Mifflin.

> Uh-ohs are common in a toddler's day. Isadora's hardcover book uses simple text to tell the story of the many mishaps a child can have. Add more description and conversation to talk with children about the adventures of the toddler in the book and relate them to the experiences of children in your class.

Kalan, Robert. 1989. *Jump, Frog, Jump!* New York: Greenwillow.

> Children will quickly learn the repeated phrase, "Jump, frog, jump!" Encourage them to join in, and point to the words to help make the connection. This is a cumulative story. If it is too long to hold their interest, stop and finish it later.

Smee, Nicola. 2007. *Clip-Clop.* St. Albans, UK: Boxer Books.

> There are a couple of repeated phrases in this book that children will quickly pick up on. After a few readings, children will repeat, "Clip-clop, clippity-clop," as well as, "Up you get," as each animal asks for a ride on Mr. Horse. The animals—Cat and Dog and Pig and Duck—are listed in the same order each time. Provide cues by pointing to each animal, and children can also repeat the names of the animals as they ride, squeal, fly through the air, and ride again.

Weeks, Sarah. 2006. *Overboard!* New York: Harcourt.

> Dropping items for you to pick up is a favorite game for young children. Once they have mastered the ability to voluntarily drop objects, they delight in dropping them over and over again. Weeks's little bunny sends many objects overboard from the high chair, bath tub, and crib. Children will love the rhyming text, fun words such as *splat* and *plink*, as well as the repetition of "Overboard!"

How to Read It: *Clip-Clop* by Nicola Smee

- This book can be read with a lot of expression. Practice before reading it with the children. You can read faster at times, slower, loudly, and with more excitement as the story builds. This will build excitement while you are reading and support print motivation.

- Encourage children to make the sounds of the animals in the book. You can do this before reading the book, which helps children to begin developing predicting skills. This supports talking, phonological awareness, and background knowledge.

- Add a horse puppet to this story. Give the puppet a voice, and he can say, "Up you get," each time an animal asks for a ride. You can also demonstrate the pace of the story by having the horse move faster and faster. Varying the pace of the story or repeated phrases is one way to keep children's interest.

- Give each animal a voice when you are reading. By changing your tone and pitch, you will keep children's attention longer. Encourage children if they try to mimic the voices of the animals. This supports talking and print motivation.

- Even though the story does not include animal sounds, you can add them. After each animal asks for a ride, add its sound. For example you can say, "'Me, please,' says Cat, 'Meow, meow,'" and "'I want a ride, too, please, Mr. Horse,' says Dog, 'Ruff, ruff.'" This will help children make connections between the animals and their sounds and will support talking and phonological awareness.

- When the animals say, "Again!" add more information. You can explain that the animals are excited to ride again and they had a great time even though they fell off. This supports talking and vocabulary development.

- When children are familiar with the story, encourage them to say the names of the animals each time they are listed. They appear in the same order each time, which makes it easier for children to learn which comes first, next, and last. This supports talking, background knowledge, vocabulary development, and oral language.

Storybooks with Few or No Words

Even books that do not have any words or have just one or two words on a page can still tell a story. They depend on you to add the expression and conversation. Wordless books help build listening skills, vocabulary, comprehension, and story structure. If storytelling is not your strength, wordless books are a great prompt. The illustrations help you tell the story. Be creative and have fun!

Alborough, Jez. 2001. *Hug*. Somerville, MA: Candlewick Press.

> A baby chimpanzee is looking for his mother and a hug. The story is told through the facial expressions and body language that the illustrations evoke.

Crews, Donald. 1991. *Truck*. New York: Greenwillow.

> The stories about the cross-country journey of this truck are only limited by your imagination. The story can be different every time you read this book.

Day, Alexandra. 1996. *Good Dog, Carl*. New York: Little Simon.

> The story starts with one simple sentence. The rest is up to the storyteller and child to create and describe the adventures of a dog babysitting a child.

Rathman, Peggy. 1996. *Good Night, Gorilla*. New York: Putnam Juvenile.

> The zookeeper is ready to put everyone to bed, but the animals have other ideas! The text is very short and simple, but the story can go on and on.

How to Read It: *Good Night, Gorilla* by Peggy Rathman

This favorite story is available in board book, lap-size board book, hardcover, and paperback. As with other books that come in a variety of formats, choose the size that works best for your purposes. If children are not ready to handle paper pages, keep the hardcover and paperback versions put up for your use with the children. The lap-size board book works well for reading to a small group of children.

- This book is good for repeated readings. You can change your focus each time: focus on the animals, talking about each one and giving additional information about them; focus on the colors and shapes in the book, talking about the red balloon and its shape, the colored squares under the cages, and the colors and patterns on the animals. This supports talking and background knowledge.

- The illustrations in this book have a lot of detail, if you look closely. Use them to encourage children to find repeated items. The mouse is on every two-page spread; help children look for it. Each animal has a stuffed animal in his cage—see if you can find them. This can spark a conversation with children about whether or not they sleep with stuffed animals. This supports talking and background knowledge.

- Introduce the concepts of *first*, *next*, and *last*. You can say, "The gorilla let the elephant out first. Next he let out the lion. Next, he let out the hyena and the giraffe. He let the armadillo out last." This will help children begin to learn story structure and supports talking, vocabulary development, and background knowledge.
- Make stuffed animals available for children to play with. They can line the animals up, put them to bed, carry them around, and sneak like the animals in the book. This is a fun way for them to reenact or retell the story. This supports play and background knowledge.
- Add a puppet to the story. The zookeeper puppet can help you tell the story. Give him a voice as he is saying good night to each of the animals. This will help keep children interested and supports reading and print motivation.

Story Time with Older Toddlers and Twos: Getting from Here to There

There are many ways to share storybooks with young children. Because you are with the same children every day, you are in a great position to reread storybooks in a variety of ways over time. Children need repetition to become familiar with the books. Also, as children grow, it is heartening to see how they come to understand the stories on increasingly complex levels. The way you share these books with children is critical to their language development and comprehension.

- Use the same song to start your story time. This helps establish routine and phonological awareness. Children will learn very quickly that this cue means that books are next. Try the following song, or any song that you like.

  Story Time Is Here

  (Sung to the tune of "The Farmer in the Dell.")

  Story time is here.

  Story time is here.

  Hey-ho, the derry-o,

  Story time is here.

  Shake your hands up high.

  Shake your hands down low.

  Hey-ho, the derry-o,

  Shake 'em high and low.

  Chorus

  Tap your feet like this.

  Tap your feet like that.

  Hey-ho, the derry-o,

  Give yourselves a pat.

Chorus

Give your hands a clap.

Give your hands a clap.

Hey-ho the derry-o,

Now put them in your lap.

- Offer a description of the theme based on the age of the children in your class. Keep this very short and concise: "Today, we are going to read some books about getting from one place to another." Or you can simply say, "It's story time!" This supports print awareness and print motivation.

- Sing a song related to the theme. You can write short songs on a large piece of paper. Add a picture of a caboose, and hold the paper up as you sing the song. This visual aid helps children make the connection between written words and songs.

Little Red Caboose

Little red caboose, chug, chug, chug.

Little red caboose, chug, chug, chug.

Little red caboose behind the train, train, train, train.

Smokestack on its back, back, back, back.

Running down the track, track, track, track.

Little red caboose behind the train.

Woo! Woo!

- Read a book related to the theme, such as *My Car* by Byron Barton. This story of Sam and his car has a lot of information in it. Talking with children, especially as you share books, is one of the best ways to develop their vocabulary. You can explain new words or pictures of things the children might not otherwise see. Talking with them about the pictures in a book is a great way to help their vocabularies grow. Good readers know lots of words!

- Sing another song related to the theme, such as "The Wheels on the Bus." By adding movement and motion to songs, young children use their whole bodies. This helps them internalize and understand what is happening. It is also a lot of fun and will capture their attention. You can add flannel story pieces and put the matching pieces up as you sing the song.

The Wheels on the Bus

(Adjust the number of verses to the attention level of your group.)

The wheels on the bus go 'round and 'round, (move your hands and arms around in a circle)

'Round and 'round, 'round and 'round.

The wheels on the bus go 'round and 'round

All through the town.

The door on the bus goes open and shut, (open your hands on *open*, clap them together on *shut*)

Open and shut, open and shut.

The door on the bus goes open and shut

All through the town.

The wipers on the bus go swish, swish, swish, (move your arms back and forth like windshield wipers)

Swish, swish, swish. Swish, swish, swish.

The wipers on the bus go swish, swish, swish

All through the town.

The horn on the bus goes beep, beep, beep, (pretend to honk the horn)

Beep, beep, beep. Beep, beep, beep.

The horn on the bus goes beep, beep, beep

All through the town.

The people on the bus go up and down, (bounce up and down)

Up and down, up and down.

The people on the bus go up and down

All through the town.

The babies on the bus go wah, wah, wah, (place your hands by your eyes and pretend to cry)

Wah, wah, wah. Wah, wah, wah.

The babies on the bus go wah, wah, wah

All through the town.

The mommies on the bus go shhh, shhh, shhh, (place your finger in front of your mouth on *shhh*)

Shhh, shhh, shhh. Shhh, shhh, shhh.

The mommies on the bus go shhh, shhh, shhh

All through the town.

- Background knowledge is information that children learn and gain through experience. In *Tractor, Tractor!* by David Bedford, children learn about opposites. Researchers have found that it is easier for children with strong background knowledge to understand what they read when they are older. It starts now! There are many ways you can develop children's background knowledge as you sing, talk, read, write, and play with them every day.

- Sing another song related to the theme.

  Merrily We Stroll Along

  Merrily we stroll along, (walk in place)

  Stroll along, stroll along.

  Merrily we stroll along,

  Waving to our friends. (wave)

- Read another book related to the theme, such as *Silly Sally* by Audrey Wood. Add flannel story pieces if you wish. Rhyming is one way that children learn to hear that words are made up of smaller parts. By reading rhyming books with them, you are supporting phonological awareness. This skill helps them when they later try to sound out words to read. And it's fun, too.

- Just as with an opening song, singing the same closing song at the end of each story time signals to the children that story time is over. This song offers a smooth transition into the next activity.

  Story Time Is Over Now

  Story time is over now,

  Over now, over now.

  Story time is over now.

  It's time to _____ . (Fill in the blank with the next activity.)

Chapter 6

Putting It into Practice

So far, you have read a lot of information about how you can use books in your classroom in ways that will help build a strong early literacy foundation for infants and toddlers. You have probably noticed that you are already doing many things to support early literacy. We hope that the items in this chapter will help you as you put more ideas into practice. You may use the information to enhance your story times or in using a particular book.

The best place to start is with a story time you have already planned. Choose one that you have done and feel comfortable with. If you want to focus on using tips and strategies with one book, select a book that you are familiar with and have read to children before.

To build on your own story time and intentionally emphasize early literacy practices and components, use the "Story-Time Planning Sheet" in Appendix A. (See Figure 6.1 for a completed sample.) Use a story time you enjoy. Choose a component, practice, or aspect of a component to emphasize during your story time. Decide what you will do to emphasize the component or practice. In the planning sheet's first column, list the title of the book, song, or rhyme. In the second column, write down your notes and reminders. In the third column, list any materials that you will need. You can use this tool for planning activities around a single book, a song, a rhyme, or another literacy activity.

> **TIP**
>
> Make these tools work for you. The purpose is not to increase the amount of paperwork you have to do but to help you be more intentional about early literacy activities. The notes you make on the sheets are to help you stay on track; they are not intended to be a script that you say to the children. On the other hand, this may be information you want to pass on to parents about what you are doing with the children and why.

Story-Time Planning Sheet

You may find it easiest to highlight just one component and practice, or even an aspect of a component, during the story time. All story times should model print motivation. The enjoyment of books and reading should always be apparent to the children. Choose one or two components from the list. Depending on what you want to accomplish, you can focus on aspects of a component. For planning purposes, background knowledge is broken into print motivation and narrative skills. Although every story time may include all components or practices, you will not emphasize every one in every story time.

Fill in your story-time plan in the order you intend to do it. You may modify your plan depending on ways you highlight a component or to adjust for the needs of that particular day. Choose a component or practice that you want to highlight. Fill in your notes related to the practice or component, and remember to include any family connections.

Figure 6.1: Sample Planning Sheet

☒ Print motivation: Enjoyment of books

☐ Phonological awareness:

    ☐ Rhyming

    ☐ Rhythm

    ☐ Playing with silly or nonsense words

☐ Print awareness:

    ☐ With books

    ☐ In the environment

☒ Vocabulary:

    ☒ Introducing new words

    ☐ Explaining (not replacing) words

    ☐ Adding less familiar words for description, action, feelings, concepts, and ideas

☐ Narrative skills:

    ☐ Encourage children to respond to simple questions

    ☐ Encourage children to repeat a word or phrase

    ☐ Ask questions about the story

    ☐ Use props, such as flannel story pieces or puppets

☐ Letter knowledge:

    ☐ Same and different

    ☐ Shapes

    ☐ Opposites

    ☐ Colors

☐ Practices:

    ☐ Read

    ☐ Write

    ☐ Sing

    ☒ Talk

    ☐ Play

Figure 6.1 (continued)

Story-Time Activity	Early Literacy Connections and Notes	Materials Needed
Opening Song: "If You Want to Hear a Story"	Make sure all story-time materials are together in the reading area.	
Introduction	Remind the children that we have been talking a lot about farm animals. Pigs live on a farm.	
Songs/Rhymes: "To Market To Market," "The Itsy Bitsy Spider"	Remember to point to the pictures as we are saying the words. Clap. The children *love* "The Itsy Bitsy Spider"!	Write words to rhyme on large paper and paste pictures of pigs.
Book: *Baby Pig: Time to Play* by Laura Gates Galvin	<ul><li>New words: *hay, trots, path, patch.*</li><li>Explain that rolling in the dirt or mud helps pigs cool off when the weather is hot.</li><li>Skip a page or so if they are getting restless!</li><li>Bring out the pig puppet to talk to them. Let the puppet ask them questions: "What color am I?" "Where do I live?"</li></ul>	Pig puppet, book
Song/Rhyme: "Three Little Ducks Went Out to Play"	Use the flannel board with this song. Start with three. They had a hard time with six when we tried it on Monday.	Flannel board, three flannel ducks
Book: *Perfect Piggies!* by Sandra Boynton	Download the song, and play it while using the book. Let them get up and dance!	Book, song on flash drive or computer, speakers
Closing song: "Story Time Is Over Now"	Make sure the other teachers are ready to help children move from story time to washing hands to get ready for snack.	

Story-Time Ideas and Book Sharing for Each Component

The following table offers samples of early literacy connections and ideas for the types of materials and activities that support each of the early literacy components. It is possible, really, to connect any book to any of the early literacy components. It is also true that some books lend themselves to one component more than another. The fourth column offers some guidelines for characteristics of books that lend themselves well to a particular early literacy component. The last column notes interactions and activities that support each component. These suggestions are samples to get you started. Use your own ideas, too!

Component or Skill	Description	Ideas for Story Time	Book Characteristics	Book Sharing
Phonological awareness	• Rhyming • Playing with words; silly, nonsense words • Animal sounds • Environmental sounds	• Use books that rhyme • Point out some rhyming words • Use Mother Goose or other rhymes • Use poetry • Sing songs and repeat them • Clap the syllables of the children's names • Clap while you sing • Encourage children to say a repeated phrase in a story • Play around with silly or nonsense words • Make animal sounds • Make environmental sounds	Any book, but particularly books with rhyme, books with alliteration, books with sounds of animals and other items, books you can sing, Mother Goose rhymes, and poetry	• Encourage children to repeat rhymes and sing songs. • Read books that have a lot of sounds in them, such as those about cars, trucks, animals, and trains.
Print Motivation	Joy of and interest in reading and books	• Model the fun of reading and of playing with language • Enjoy the book and the interaction yourself • Keep children involved • Have children join in at appropriate parts • Use information books • Have a comfortable setting where children share time talking about and looking at books	Any book, but particularly books that you and the children love.	• Keep the interaction around the book reading and sharing positive and enjoyable. • Keep the children involved, even if it means not reading the book word for word. • Remember that a child's age, stage, and personality affect how she interacts with books. • Respond to the children and their mood.
Vocabulary	• Introduce new words. • Explain (do not replace) unfamiliar words. • Use words that label or explain rather than using *this, that, here,* and *there.*	• Pick out a word from a book, rhyme, or song. For an unfamiliar word, explain; for a familiar word, introduce a less familiar word. • Add descriptive words. • Have children repeat less familiar words. • Use information books as a source of new words. • Bring in the real items of pictures shown in the book. • Ask questions, and pause to give children time to respond, even if the response is babbling, cooing, or gestures.	Any book, but particularly information books and books with words not typically used in daily conversation	• Explain an unfamiliar word; do not replace it with a familiar one. • Pick out a word from a book, rhyme, or song. For an unfamiliar word, explain it. For a familiar word, tell children a less familiar word. • Add descriptive words or more information to what is in the book. • Have children repeat unfamiliar words. • Encourage children to talk about the pictures, and add information and ideas to what they say. • Talk about the feelings that characters in the book might be feeling, even if those words are not used in the book. • Talk about ideas in the book even if the words for those ideas are not actually used in the book.

Component or Skill	Description	Ideas for Story Time	Book Characteristics	Book Sharing
Narrative Skills	Retelling stories or retelling events	• Have children say repeated words along with you as you read the book. • Have children do a motion as they repeat a phrase along with you. • Repeat reading books but with a different theme to bring out different aspects of the stories. • Retell a story with puppets, flannel-board pieces, props, or creative dramatics. • Ask questions.	Any book, but particularly books with a repeated phrase, repetition, or a sequence	• Encourage participation, saying a repeated phrase together. • Reread books so that children can become familiar with the stories, making it easier to retell them. • Have children tell or retell a story. • Encourage children to tell you something that they remember that is related to what happens in a book. • Encourage children to play with props such as puppets. • Retell familiar stories with props or other aids that will help children remember the order of the story. • Talk about the pictures in the book. • Encourage children to draw pictures and tell you about them.
Print Awareness	• Beginning to understand that print has meaning • Knowing how to handle a book • Beginning to understand that we read text, not pictures • Learning that in English we read from left to right and top to bottom • Beginning to recognize that print is all around us	• Run your finger under the title and any repeated phrase. • Write out rhymes or songs on flipcharts or cards. • Talk about environmental print: point out signs, labels, logos, and so on. • Include books with signs in the images and varying print orientations, such as *Truck.* • Point out when pictures show signs or print around them. • Start with books oriented the wrong way, and let the children correct you	Any book, but some books have writing as part of the pictures, such as *Hi, Pizza Man!* by Virginia Walter	• Point to the words of the title as you say them. • Let children turn the pages of the book. • Point to the words in a repeated phrase as you say them. • Play around with the orientation of the book. Start with it upside down. Tell the children you are turning it around so you can read it. • Encourage scribbling.
Letter Knowledge	• Beginning to understand that letters have names and represent sounds • Knowing concepts such as shapes and *alike* and *different*	• Point out and talk about shapes. • Let children feel different shapes. • Give opportunities for children to match and sort and see how things are alike and different, such as sorting toys to put them away. • Provide large foam letters and blocks with letters. • Encourage children to scribble and draw. • Use variations of the "B-I-N-G-O" song. • Make a variety of textures available, and describe the textures. • Point out and talk about colors.	Any book, but particularly books with shapes or textures or books about colors	• With any book, not necessarily an alphabet book, you can point out a letter. • Show a child the first letter in his name. Look for that letter in the book. • Encourage scribbling, drawing, and writing.

Reflection, Observation, and Evaluation

Now that you have a plan, it is time to implement it. If you really want to challenge yourself to increase the focus on early literacy, you need to go further. As you begin to incorporate more literacy-rich activities into your day, you will want to determine if what you are doing is working. One way to review what you have done and to evaluate your success is to reflect on what you did. This does not have to be a long, involved process. You can write down your thoughts and observations. Ask yourself some questions, such as the following.

- Did it work? How do I know? (What did you see?)
- What did the children do? (Sat through the entire book, repeated new words, did the motions of a song, batted at a page, and so on.)
- What behaviors did I see that I have not seen before? (The children looked at pictures I pointed to, turned the page, babbled back when I paused after a question, and so on.)
- Did I enjoy the book or activity?
- Would I read this book again or do this activity again? Why or why not?
- Did I include new vocabulary?

The checklists can be used for reflection and self-observation. Feel free to replicate them and use them in any way that is supportive to enhancing early literacy in your classroom. Make notes about specific children, such as Marissa pointed to the pictures, Sasha turned the pages, or Dominic babbled back to me.

Letter Knowledge
Knowing that the same letter can look different and that letters have names and are related to sounds

In the Classroom with Infants

- ☐ I read information books with the babies and make sure there are a lot of information books available in the classroom.
- ☐ I encourage babies to play with different kinds of toys. I talk with them about the toys, such as describing the shape of the rattle and the colors of the soft blocks.
- ☐ I choose books that have sharp contrast, such as black on white or books with colorful and clear photographs, which are easier for babies to see.
- ☐ I describe what a baby is looking at—the color, shape, and texture—so that later she will learn to notice these characteristics.
- ☐ I encourage parents to visit the library with their children and check out books to share.

In the Classroom with Toddlers

☐ I read information books with the children and make sure there are a lot of information books available in the classroom.

☐ When I play with toddlers, I talk with them about the toys, describing the shapes and colors of the blocks, balls, cars, dolls, and so on.

☐ I describe an item that a toddler is interested in—color, shape, texture—and how the items she is playing with are alike and different.

☐ I choose books that have sharp contrast, clear pictures, and bright colors. I take time to describe what is in the pictures and encourage children to talk about them, too.

☐ I play with puzzles with toddlers, encouraging them to turn the pieces until they fit.

☐ Outside, I talk with toddlers about similarities and differences, such as how the sand feels different from the grass or how the color of a flower is the same as their shirt.

☐ I use daily opportunities, such as sorting blocks to put away, to have toddlers help me match things.

☐ I look at books with toddlers, sometimes mentioning the names of the letters and talking about the pictures.

☐ When writing a toddler's name, I make sure to use both uppercase and lowercase letters.

☐ I take time to play sorting games with toddlers, such as sorting cars or doll clothes.

☐ I encourage toddlers to scribble and talk about what the scribble says.

☐ I encourage parents to visit the library with their toddlers and check out books to share together.

Background Knowledge: Narrative Skills

Ability to describe things and events, to tell and retell stories

In the Classroom with Infants

☐ I read simple stories to the babies and make sure there are a lot of storybooks available in the classroom.

☐ When I talk to babies, I allow time for them to babble back to me.

☐ When I use lots of different facial expressions with babies, I notice that they react to what I am saying.

☐ I realize that babies are communicating with me by using gestures, such as waving, pointing, nodding, and clapping, pushing food or drink away, or lifting arms to be picked up.

☐ I narrate my day to the babies, saying what I am doing as I do it or saying what they are doing. I wait for babies to talk to me, too.

☐ I say nursery rhymes to the children, repeating the rhymes and encouraging them to say them, too.

☐ I share books with the babies, talking about the pictures, encouraging them to talk about the pictures, too.

☐ I ask *what* questions when we look at pictures in a book or magazine. Then I say what the picture is and give the children time to imitate me.

☐ Even if I get tired of singing songs, saying nursery rhymes, and reading books over and over again, I still do it because it helps babies learn.

☐ I encourage parents to visit the library with their children.

In the Classroom with Toddlers

☐ I read stories to the children and make sure there are a lot of storybooks available in the classroom.

☐ When I talk with toddlers, I allow time for them to talk back. This may be from five to twelve seconds.

☐ When a toddler is communicating with me by using gestures, I say the words and encourage him to say them as well.

☐ The more I repeat a nursery rhyme and do some actions, the more the children try to say the words.

☐ I use pictures, flannel-board figures, stuffed animals, or puppets as I say nursery rhymes or tell stories, and I encourage toddlers to say the words themselves.

☐ The more I sing with the children, the more they are remembering and able to sing the song (even if I cannot understand all of their words).

☐ When I read books with a toddler, I include a repeated phrase that they can try to say.

☐ When I read books with toddlers, I do not worry if I cannot finish the book. I know that listening to what a child is saying about the pictures is helping to develop narrative skills.

☐ When I read books with toddlers, I ask *what* questions, wait for a response, and add more words. I encourage them to repeat what I say, but I do not force it.

☐ Even if I get tired of singing songs, saying animal sounds, saying nursery rhymes, and reading books over and over again, I still do it because it helps toddlers learn.

☐ I encourage parents to visit the library with their children.

Phonological Awareness

Ability to hear and play with the smaller sounds in words

In the Classroom with Infants

☐ I read and sing books and rhymes with the children and make books you can sing and nursery rhyme books available in the classroom.

☐ When I talk with a baby, she tries to imitate my words.

☐ When I say the sounds of animals, she listens.

☐ When I say the sounds of animals, she tries to imitate the sounds.

☐ I use flannel-board pictures, stuffed animals, toys, or puppets to talk about the sounds of the animals.

☐ The more I talk with babies, the more I notice them babbling back and saying more sounds.

☐ When I say or sing nursery rhymes, such as "Hickory Dickory Dock," and do some actions with them, the children respond with interest.

☐ When I sing to a baby, he shows enjoyment.

☐ The more I sing with the children, the more I notice them trying to imitate me.

- ☐ Babies enjoy it when I hold them and dance in rhythm to music.
- ☐ When I shake the shaker in rhythm to music or a rhyme, the children are alert to the sound.
- ☐ I share board books with babies, talking about the pictures and the sounds of the animals.
- ☐ Even if I get tired of singing songs, saying animal sounds, saying nursery rhymes, and reading books over and over again, I still do it because it helps babies learn.
- ☐ I encourage parents to visit the library with their children.

In the Classroom with Toddlers

- ☐ I read and sing books and rhymes with the children and make books you can sing and nursery rhyme books available in the classroom.
- ☐ When I talk with toddlers, they try to imitate what I say.
- ☐ When I say the sounds of animals, toddlers repeat those sounds.
- ☐ When I ask a toddler what sound an animal makes, he answers with the sound of an animal (sometimes correctly).
- ☐ When I use the flannel-board pictures, stuffed animals, toys, or puppets to talk about the sounds of the animals, the children play with the items and try to say the sounds of the animals.
- ☐ The more I repeat a nursery rhyme, such as "Hickory Dickory Dock," and do some actions, the more the children try to say the words and hear the rhythm and rhyme.
- ☐ When I sing with a toddler, she sings some of the words, too.
- ☐ The more I sing with a toddler, the more she is remembering and able to sing the song (even if I cannot understand the words).
- ☐ When I sing with toddlers or play rhythmic music, they move to the rhythm.
- ☐ When we sing songs or play music, we use shakers or clap to emphasize the beat of the music.
- ☐ I read board books with toddlers, talking about the pictures and the sounds of the animals.
- ☐ Even if I get tired of singing songs, saying animal sounds, saying nursery rhymes, and reading books over and over again, I still do it because it helps toddlers learn.

Background Knowledge: Print Motivation

A child's interest in and enjoyment of books and reading

In the Classroom with Infants

- ☐ I read and play with interactive books and encourage the children to lift the flaps, look through holes, and feel the textures.
- ☐ When a baby chews or bites on a book, I gently take it out of her mouth and talk about the pictures.
- ☐ I share books when a baby is not too tired and not too active but quietly alert.
- ☐ I choose books with bright colors and high contrast, which are more likely to keep a baby's attention.
- ☐ I read in a cheerful voice.
- ☐ I keep books handy in all areas of the room, including near the changing table, and with toys, so it is easy to share books with babies everywhere.
- ☐ When the babies get fussy, I know I can continue reading another time.

☐ Even if I get tired of singing songs, saying nursery rhymes, and reading books over and over again, I still do it because it helps babies learn.

☐ I encourage parents to visit the library with their children and to check out books to share.

In the Classroom with Toddlers

☐ I read and play with interactive books and encourage the children to lift the flaps, look through holes, and feel the textures.

☐ I give toddlers choices when reading books together.

☐ I try to make sharing books with toddlers a special and enjoyable time.

☐ I keep the children engaged by encouraging them to participate as we read the book.

☐ I keep books handy in all areas of the room, including near the changing table, and with toys, so it is easy to share books anytime.

☐ When a toddler loses interest in a book, I do not turn it into a power struggle. I can pick up the book another time.

☐ I look for books on topics that the children are interested in.

☐ Even if I get tired of singing songs, saying animal sounds, saying nursery rhymes, and reading books over and over again, I still do it because it helps toddlers learn.

☐ I encourage parents to visit the library with their children and check out books to share together.

Print Awareness

Understanding that print has meaning, knowing how to handle a book, understanding the direction of print, noticing print all around us

In the Classroom with Infants

☐ When a baby bites or chews on books, I realize this is how babies are getting to know books and how they work. I gently take the book from the baby's mouth and talk about the pictures. I give him a rattle or something else to chew on.

☐ I encourage babies to turn the pages in a book, even though their hands may just bat at the pages.

☐ I point to pictures as I say the words.

☐ From time to time, I point to the text on the pages of a book as I say the words.

☐ Because babies learn through their senses, when possible I show them the real item as I point out the picture in a book.

☐ When we are out walking or outside playing, I point out signs and tell them what they say.

☐ I encourage parents to visit the library with their children and check out books to share.

In the Classroom with Toddlers

☐ I encourage toddlers to turn the pages in a book, and I help when needed.

☐ I point to pictures as I say the words.

☐ From time to time, I point to the text on the pages of a book as I say the words. This helps toddlers understand that the written word represents what I am saying.

- ☐ Young children learn through their senses, so when possible I show toddlers the real item as I point out the picture in the book.
- ☐ When I read books with toddlers, I point to the words in the title and in repeated phrases as I read them.
- ☐ When a toddler hands me a book upside down or backwards, I talk about starting the book at the front.
- ☐ When we are out walking or outside playing, I point out signs and tell the toddlers what they say.
- ☐ I let toddlers see me writing a note and then tell them what it says.
- ☐ When I write a list, I read it to the children, pointing to the words and telling them why I wrote the list.
- ☐ I encourage toddlers to draw and then talk about the picture.
- ☐ I encourage toddlers to scribble and talk about what it says.
- ☐ I encourage parents to visit the library with their children and check out books to share together.

Vocabulary

Knowing the names of things, concepts, feelings, and ideas

In the Classroom with Infants

- ☐ I read a lot of information books and make them available in the classroom.
- ☐ When I talk to babies, I use parentese: a higher pitch; short, simple sentences; and long vowel sounds.
- ☐ When I use lots of different facial expressions with babies, I notice that they will listen to me longer. I know they learn more from my talking with them than from watching TV or DVDs.
- ☐ Even when I speak to a baby in parentese, I use big words.
- ☐ I narrate the day to babies, saying what I am doing as I do it or saying what they are doing.
- ☐ I say and sing nursery rhymes, such as "Hickory Dickory Dock," and do some actions as I say them, because that is one way babies learn new words.
- ☐ I share books with babies, talking about the pictures.
- ☐ When I read books with babies, I use big words, both the ones in the book and words I add.
- ☐ If I am reading materials myself, I read some of it aloud to the children.
- ☐ When I talk with babies, I notice how they react with different expressions in their eyes and faces.
- ☐ Even if I get tired of singing songs, saying nursery rhymes, and reading books over and over again, I still do it because it helps babies learn.
- ☐ I encourage parents to visit the library with their children.

In the Classroom with Toddlers

- ☐ I read a lot of information books and make them available in the classroom.
- ☐ I narrate the day to toddlers, saying what I am doing as I do it or saying what a child is doing
- ☐ I try to find ways to encourage toddlers rather than just saying no, by offering choices, explaining reasons, talking about feelings, and using words for self-control such as *wait* or *gently*.

☐ The more I repeat a nursery rhyme and do some actions, the more the children try to say the words.

☐ The more I sing with toddlers, the more they remember and are able to sing the song (even if I cannot understand all their words).

☐ As I talk with a toddler, I use words a toddler does not understand yet. I know they learn more from my talking with them than from watching TV or DVDs.

☐ When a toddler talks to me, I repeat what she says and then add some more words.

☐ Even if a toddler does not understand, that does not stop me—I explain what words mean or talk about what is going on around us.

☐ When I read books with toddlers, I ask *what* questions and add more words.

☐ When I read books with toddlers, I add words that they do not know.

☐ Even if I get tired of singing songs, saying nursery rhymes, and reading books over and over again, I still do it because it helps toddlers learn.

☐ I encourage parents to visit the library with their children and check out books to share together.

Another way to get feedback on how you are doing is to have someone observe you as you implement early literacy strategies. You can ask a coteacher, administrator, mentor, or other staff person to watch what you are doing and give you feedback. Use the following Early Literacy Checklist.

Figure 6.2: Early Literacy Checklist

Ages: Birth through 24 Months

Date: **Teacher:**   **Observer:**

Story-Time Observation	Notes
Section 1: Beginning ☐ Story time is conducted in a designated place (if appropriate) ☐ Is prepared to begin story time ☐ Initiates story time with an opening activity or song ☐ Uses an activity to allow children to move before being expected to sit for story time, if necessary **Section 2: Background Knowledge: Print Motivation, Narrative Skills, and Prior Knowledge** ☐ Conveys the idea that reading is fun ☐ Reads a developmentally appropriate book ☐ Selects a book that has good clear pictures or illustrations ☐ Uses voice tone and expression to make story time interesting ☐ Helps children link the activity and book to experiences familiar to them ☐ Uses puppets, props, flannel-board pieces, or a story apron during story time ☐ Reviews events of the story or theme ☐ Talks with children, asks questions, uses predictions, and allows time for children to respond **Section 3: Phonological Awareness** ☐ Uses music and songs ☐ Invites and encourages children to chime in on rhymes, fingerplays, songs, and poems ☐ Emphasizes rhyming words ☐ Adds actions and movements to songs and poems ☐ Uses silly or nonsense songs ☐ Uses books and activities that highlight sound awareness, such as animal sounds, transportation, and so on	

Story-Time Observation	Notes

Section 4: Vocabulary and Oral Language

☐ Makes connections between pictures and real things or people

☐ Calls attention to the pictures in the story

☐ Repeats rhymes, songs, and phrases in books

☐ Exposes children to vocabulary and explains vocabulary they may not be familiar with

☐ Uses full sentences when adding information and avoids just labeling

☐ Uses voice to support meaning

Section 5: Print Awareness

☐ Holds book so children can see text and pictures

☐ Points to the print or pictures intermittently while reading

☐ Occasionally runs finger along text while reading

☐ Demonstrates how to correctly handle a book by reading left to right, turning pages, and holding book upright

☐ Calls attention to the cover of the book; points out or talks about the title and author

Section 6: Letter Knowledge

☐ Talks about what is the same and different between things

☐ Uses an enjoyable alphabet or concept book, activity, or song

☐ Points to and names shapes, colors, and so on

☐ Uses objects to teach shapes, colors, and so on

Section 7: Ending and Overall Observations

☐ Transitions from story time with a closing activity

☐ Practice is evident

☐ Uses positive behavior management techniques

☐ Changes activities as necessary

Chapter 7

Connecting with Parents and Families

Encouraging early literacy at home makes a big difference for the children in your classroom. Sharing your knowledge about early literacy practices and components will benefit the families and children. We have included sample parent letters to give you ideas of how you can share information about early literacy components and practices. Feel free to replicate these letters or create your own. You can even take sections of the letters to use in newsletters, create flyers to send home or post in the classroom, incorporate into bulletin boards, or use as talking points with parents. Additionally, we have included sample Parent Tips. Each focuses on a different skill for infants or toddlers. These are very similar to the self-observation tool from Chapter 6. Feel free to share these tips with families.

Sample Letters

Dear Parent,

Children need a lot of skills to become good readers. Even though your child is very young, you can help by building those skills now. Narrative skills, or the ability to describe things and events and to tell stories, are an important part of later literacy. For infants and toddlers, this means helping them to use expressive language such as babbling, repeating a word or phrase, or trying to tell you what is happening. These all lead to better comprehension and understanding later.

We will be reading books and asking the children lots of questions here at school. We would like to invite you to join us in this effort by doing some of the following things at home with your child:

● When you talk with your child, pause and give him or her time to respond to you. Even if the child is not talking yet or only has a few words, give him or her time to babble or coo. This helps your child learn that conversations go back and forth.
● Read storybooks from the library or use the books you have at home. After you read a story, ask your child questions about what happens in the story.
● Talk about what you are doing throughout the day.
● Read every day with your child.

We have many fun projects to work on with the children. One of our goals for the year is to make sure that all of the children are ready to go to school knowing what they need to know to become good readers. We are grateful for your support and for your willingness to work with us on this important task. Please let us know if you have any questions.

Sincerely,

Dear Parent,

Before children can learn to read, they need to learn a lot about reading. You can help your child now even though he or she won't start reading for quite a while. A skill he or she will need to learn to read is letter knowledge, which is learning to name letters and to recognize them everywhere.

Letter knowledge is knowing that letters are different from one another and that they can look different ways. It is also knowing that letters represent sounds. Learning about the ABCs begins early. To learn about letters, children have to understand some basic concepts first. Researchers *have found that children identify letters by their shapes. Helping children learn shapes helps them recognize letters. Other concepts that lead to letter knowledge are knowing about opposites, similarities and differences, and even colors. All of these concepts come into play when determining the difference between one letter and another. Your child will learn these skills more quickly with your help. Here are some things that you can do:*

- *Point out and talk about shapes and colors.*
- *Describe textures.*
- *Read books that include shapes and colors.*
- *Sing songs with letters in them, such as "B-I-N-G-O."*
- *Make comparisons. Talk about what is the same and different in how two objects look.*

You are your child's first and most important teacher. Remember to have fun and to change activities before you or child become frustrated. As always, we appreciate your support! Let us know if there is anything we can do to help you help your child as he or she gains the skills needed to be successful in school.

Sincerely,

Dear Parent,

In our class this week, we are paying particular attention to a reading skill called phonological awareness, which is the ability to hear and to play with the different sounds that are in the words we speak. It includes rhyming and singing. We rhyme, sing, and make lots of fun sounds every day in our classroom.

Your child will learn this skill more quickly with your help. Please play with words and their sounds as you spend time with your child. Here are some things that you can do:

- *Read books that rhyme.*
- *Say and sing nursery rhymes.*
- *Make lots of noises—animal sounds (moo moo), transportation sounds (vroom vroom), and silly sounds (splish, splash, splosh).*
- *When your baby makes sounds, repeat them.*

You are your children's first and most important teacher. As always we appreciate your support.

Sincerely,

Dear Parent,

Children are getting ready to read when they are very young. They need to learn how books work, what print is, and how to follow print on a page. The skill is called print awareness.

Your child will become more aware of print with your help. Here are some things that you can do with your child as the opportunity arises. To learn that print is everywhere:

- *Point out signs, labels, and logos.*
- *When you are doing errands with your child, point out signs of different stores that you go to.*
- *Once you are in the store, point out the sale signs and the words on the different items.*

To follow print on a page:

- *When you read a book together, point out the title and author of the book. Run your finger under both the title and the author's name.*
- *From time to time, point out the words on the page as you read them.*
- *Encourage your child to help turn the pages. This will teach him or her that in English we read from left to right. It will also teach how to hold a book.*
- *With your toddler, pretend to read the book backward, starting from the end and flipping the pages the wrong way. Ask your child what you are doing wrong!*

Have fun as you explore the world of print with your child. It is fun to watch them as they start to figure out the magic behind the written word. As always, let us know if you have any questions.

Sincerely,

Dear Parent,

Children learn very early that books are fun. They develop a love of reading and books long before they start going to school. A child's interest in and enjoyment of books is called print motivation.

Your child will acquire this skill with your help! This is a skill that takes time and patience. The most important part of teaching print motivation is done by simply reading with our children in an enjoyable way. Here are some ideas on how to take the pressure off of reading to help keep it doable and fun for you:

- *You don't have to read all of the books that your child wants at one time.*
- *You can split reading time into parts. Read one book before dinner and two before bed.*
- *Keep a lot of short, simple books on hand. Let the child choose books to read.*
- *It is okay that your child wants to hear the same book over and over. Some children memorize books and actually learn to read that way!*
- *Avoid using book-sharing time as a reward or punishment. It should be a part of your life together, just like sharing a meal.*

- *It is more important for your book-sharing time to be positive than it is for it to be long.*
- *Keep a fresh supply of books on hand. Visit your public library.*
- *Build your own home library. You can find used books in good condition at yard sales and thrift shops.*
- *Above all, have fun. Encourage your child to love books and the stories within them. Talk about your favorite stories, and repeat the rhymes. Make books a part of your lives.*

Let us know how you are doing as you make book-sharing an important part of your daily life.

Sincerely,

Dear Parent,

Young children need to hear a lot of words. This helps them learn what words mean and the names of objects, actions, feelings, concepts, and ideas. This is called vocabulary, or knowing the meanings of words. Because it is easier for children to read words that they know, it is important that they learn many, many words. The children will be learning new words at school all year long. We hope you will join us in teaching your child many new words.

Here are some things that you can do to help your child learn new words:

- *When you read together, label the names of the objects that you see in the book. Ask your child to repeat the names of new things after you have said them. If the child isn't talking yet, pause and give him or her time to respond. The response may be a gesture, such as batting at the page, or a coo.*
- *Share information books—books that include factual information. They are a good way to learn new words. Try to get books about things that are interesting to your child. Ask your librarian for some ideas if you aren't sure what to borrow.*
- *When you are doing errands together, point out new things and explain what they are and what they are used for. Use words your child does not yet know!*
- *Conversation is important! Talk, talk, and then talk some more. Point out the clouds and the shapes they make, how the rain sounds, and how you feel. The more words children hear, the more words they will know.*
- *Call things what they are. For example, if you know the name of a flower, call it by its name. Remember not to dumb things down, while still keeping things on a level the child can handle.*

We are excited that we will all be working together to make sure that all of the children are ready to go to school and ready to read! If you have any questions or concerns, please let us know.

Sincerely,

Dear Parents,

Kindergarten may seem like it is far away, but you can start getting your child ready for school now! Helping your child learn to love reading and enjoying books will make learning to read much easier when he or she is older. Reading aloud to your child is the single most important activity you can do to help him or her become a successful reader later on.

How you read to your child is just as important as how often you read. Reading the words in books is important, because sometimes books use interesting words we don't use in regular conversation. Your child needs to hear a lot of words while he or she is young.

- *Read every day!*
- *Talk about what is happening in the pictures of books.*
- *When you are reading, point to the pictures and words in the book.*
- *Have fun while you are reading: give the characters voices, read fast, read slowly, get loud, and whisper.*
- *Visit the library.*
- *Reread books that your child likes.*
- *Read books that rhyme.*
- *Sing the words in books.*

Helping your child enjoy books will go a long way when he or she is later being taught to read in school. Children who have had enjoyable experiences around books and reading are more likely to stick with learning to read even if it is difficult for them. Please let us know if you have any questions. Feel free to look around our room and see the types of books that we have.

Sincerely,

Dear Parents,

Early literacy begins with the first words you say to your baby. Talking is the basis for all later literacy. It actually helps your child get ready to learn how to read. Children need to have strong oral language and listening, speaking, and communication skills. The way we talk with children makes a big difference in their early literacy development. Talking to them from the time they are born, making eye contact, watching their gestures and responses, using words they are not familiar with all help them get ready to learn how to read.

- *Talk, talk, and talk some more.*
- *Talk about things that are not present, what has happened, and what will happen.*
- *Explain what you are doing.*

- *Ask questions that can't be answered by a simple yes or no.*
- *When you ask a question, pause and give your child time to respond, even if it is babbling or cooing.*
- *Encourage your baby to babble to you.*

Children who enter school with a large vocabulary will have an easier time understanding what they read. They will also find it easier to sound out words they have heard before. If you have any questions or concerns about ways that you can talk to your child, please ask.

Sincerely,

Dear Parents,

Children love to sing! Singing is a very important activity to do with your child. Even if you think you can't sing well, that doesn't matter—children just love it when you sing. It also helps them get ready to learn how to read. Singing slows down language; it takes us longer to sing a rhyme than to say it.

Children can hear words broken down into parts, which will help them later sound out words when they learn to read. Songs often have interesting words that we don't hear in regular conversation.

- *As you go through your day, sing with your child. It will help him or her get ready to learn how to read.*
- *Find books at the library that you can sing. Ask the librarian for assistance.*
- *Sing and read rhymes.*
- *Encourage your child to play music on the pots and pans in the kitchen.*
- *Sing along when your child makes up songs.*
- *Clap, sing, and dance together.*
- *Sing songs about what you are doing: "This is the way we wash our hands . . . ."*

Thank you for continuing to include early literacy activities at home. You are helping your child build a foundation of skills that are very important for reading success.

Sincerely,

Dear Parents,

Writing may seem like an activity for older children, but writing skills start early. Even babies like to grasp your finger! Later they will use this pincer grasp by picking up small items with their index fingers and thumbs. The small motor skills you do with babies, from clapping to songs with motions, will help develop the finger and hand movements needed for writing. There are lots of activities you can do with your child can help him or her get ready to write.

- *Encourage your child to scribble. This is the beginning of writing.*
- *Let your child see you write. Let him or her sit on your lap while you make the grocery list or write checks for bills.*
- *Let your toddler hold the grocery list while you are shopping.*
- *Encourage your child to turn the pages of books; this helps develop eye-hand coordination.*
- *Keep art supplies on hand: crayons, paper, markers, chalk, pens, fingerpaints, and pencils.*

You are your child's first and most important teacher. Have fun as you write, draw, and scribble with your child. Please let us know if you have any questions or concerns.

Sincerely,

Dear Parents,

Children learn best through play and exploration. Play is very important for children, even when they are infants. When you and your child are playing together, add more words to your conversation. Children learn words best in context, or in the moment. Pretending while you play gives you lots of opportunities to use new words. The more words your children know, the better. It is easier to read a word you know than one you don't.

- *Play with books. Children will treat them as a toy, and that is okay!*
- *Play games such as peekaboo. This helps babies learn that an object is still there even if they can't see it (object permanence). Lift-the-flap books are great for playing peekaboo.*
- *Play sorting games as you clean up. You can say, for example, "The brown wooden blocks go in this basket. The soft fuzzy blocks go on the shelf."*
- *Play with stuffed animals, dolls, and puppets. You can even retell a story with them.*
- *Let your child be the leader. Follow what he or she wants to play.*
- *Talk a lot while you are playing. Ask questions, describe things, and narrate what you or your child is doing.*

Have fun with your child, playing is not a waste of time. Your child is learning a lot and getting ready to be a reader. Please let us know if you have any questions or concerns.

Sincerely,

Parent Tips

To offer children the highest quality of care and to prepare them for later reading success, we must partner with parents and families. As early childhood professionals, we know our classroom best, but families know their children best. We need to talk with them, share our observations, and give them early literacy information. We also need to listen to what they have to say and answer their questions. If we do not know the answer, we need to find out. We are a resource for families. Together, we make a very strong team of adults who want the best for children. The Parent Tips that follow include early literacy advice and activity suggestions. You can give these tips in a newsletter or on a bulletin board or pair them with a parent letter.

Letter Knowledge

Knowing the same letter can look different and that letters have names and are related to sounds

- Encourage your baby to play with different kinds of toys. Talk with your baby about the characteristics of the toys, such as the shape of the rattle and the colors of the soft blocks.
- Choose books that have sharp contrast, such as black on white or books with colorful and clear photographs, which are easier for your baby to see.
- Describe what your baby is looking at, the color, shape, and texture so that later he or she will learn to notice these characteristics.
- Read books that include real information.
- Visit the library with your baby, and check out books to share.

You and Your Baby

☐ I encourage my baby to play with different kinds of toys. I talk with my baby about the toys, such as describing the shape of the rattle and the colors of the soft blocks.

☐ I choose books that have sharp contrast, such as black on white or books with colorful and clear photographs, which are easier for my baby to see.

☐ I describe what my baby is looking at, the color, shape, and texture, so that later my baby will learn to notice these characteristics.

☐ I visit the library with my baby and check out books to share with my baby.

You and Your Toddler

☐ Play with your toddler, and talk about the toys, such as describing the shapes and colors of the blocks, balls, cars, and dolls.

☐ Describe what your toddler is interested in, the color, shape, texture, and how the items he or she is playing with are alike and different.

☐ Read books that include real information.

☐ Choose books that have sharp contrast, clear pictures, and bright colors. Take time to describe what is in the pictures, and encourage your child to talk about them, too.

- [ ] Play with puzzles, and encourage your toddler to turn the pieces until they fit.
- [ ] At the grocery store, talk with your toddler about the similarities and differences among different foods; for example, apples come in different colors, and different cereals have similarities and differences.
- [ ] Use daily opportunities, such as matching socks when folding the laundry or stacking dishes from the dishwasher, to have your toddler help you match things.
- [ ] Look at alphabet books with your toddler, mention the names of the letters, and talk about the pictures.
- [ ] When you write your toddler's name, make sure to use both uppercase and lowercase letters.
- [ ] Take time to play sorting games, such as sorting cars or doll clothes.
- [ ] Encourage your toddler to scribble and talk about what it says.
- [ ] Visit the library with your toddler, and check out books to share together.

Narrative Skills

Ability to describe things and events, to tell and retell stories

- Talk to your baby, and allow time for him or her to babble back to you.
- Use lots of different facial expressions with your baby, and notice that your baby reacts to what you are saying. Give him or her time to babble back to you.
- Your baby is communicating with you by using gestures, such as waving, pointing, nodding, and clapping, pushing food or drink away, or lifting arms to be picked up.
- Narrate your day to your baby. Say what you are doing as you do it, or say what your baby is doing. Wait for your baby to talk back to you, too.
- Say nursery rhymes to your child, repeat them, and encourage your child to say them, too.
- Read books that have a story.
- Share books with your baby. Talk about the pictures, and encourage your baby to "talk" about the pictures, too.
- Ask *what* questions when you look at pictures in a book or magazine. Say what the picture is, and give your baby time to imitate you.
- Even if you get tired of singing songs, saying nursery rhymes, and reading books over and over again, keep doing it because it helps your baby learn.
- Visit the library with your baby.
- Talk with your toddler, and allow time for your child to talk back. This may take from five to twelve seconds.
- When your toddler is communicating with you by using gestures, say the words and encourage your child to say them as well.
- The more you repeat a nursery rhyme and do some actions, the more your toddler will try to say the words.
- Use pictures, flannel-board figures, stuffed animals, or puppets as you say nursery rhymes or tell stories, and encourage your child to say the words, too.

- The more you sing with your toddler, the more your child is remembering and able to sing the song. (You may not understand all the child's words.)
- Read books with your toddler, and include a repeated phrase that the toddler can try to say.
- Read books that have a story. Your child is learning that stories have a beginning, a middle, and an end.
- Read books with your toddler. Don't worry if you can't finish the book. Listening to what your toddler is saying about the pictures is helping to develop narrative skills.
- Ask *what* questions, wait for a response, and add more words. Encourage your child to repeat what you say, but don't force it.
- Even if you get tired of singing songs, saying animal sounds, saying nursery rhymes, and reading books over and over again, keep doing it because it helps your toddler learn.
- Visit the library with your toddler.

You and Your Baby

☐ When I talk to my baby, I allow time for my baby to babble back to me.

☐ When I use lots of different facial expressions with my baby, I notice that my baby reacts to what I am saying. I give my baby time to babble back to me.

☐ I realize that my baby is communicating with me by using gestures, such as waving, pointing, nodding, and clapping, pushing food or drink away, or lifting arms to be picked up.

☐ I narrate my day to my baby, saying what I am doing as I do it or saying what my baby is doing. I wait for my baby to talk to me, too.

☐ I say nursery rhymes to my child, repeating them, and encouraging my baby to say them, too.

☐ I share books with my baby, talking about the pictures, encouraging my baby to "talk" about the pictures, too.

☐ I ask *what* questions when we look at pictures in a book or magazine. Then I say what the picture is and give my baby time to imitate me.

☐ Even if I get tired of singing songs, saying nursery rhymes, and reading books over and over again, I still do it because it helps my baby learn.

☐ I visit the library with my baby.

You and Your Toddler

☐ When I talk with my toddler, I allow time for my toddler to talk back. This may take from five to twelve seconds.

☐ When my toddler is communicating with me by using gestures, I say the words and encourage my toddler to say them as well.

☐ The more I repeat a nursery rhyme and do some actions, the more my toddler tries to say the words.

☐ Using pictures, flannel-board figures, stuffed animals, or puppets, I say nursery rhymes or tell stories and encourage my toddler to say the words, too.

☐ The more I sing with my toddler, the more my toddler is remembering and able to sing the song (even if I cannot understand all my child's words).

- ☐ When I read books with my toddler, I include a repeated phrase that my toddler can try to say.
- ☐ When I read books with my toddler, I don't worry if I can't finish the book. I know that listening to what my toddler is saying about the pictures is helping to develop narrative skills.
- ☐ When I read books with my toddler, I ask *what* questions, wait for a response, and add more words. I encourage my child to repeat what I say, but I don't force it.
- ☐ Even if I get tired of singing songs, saying animal sounds, saying nursery rhymes, and reading books over and over again, I still do it because it helps my toddler learn.
- ☐ I visit the library with my toddler.

Phonological Awareness

Ability to hear and play with the smaller sounds in words

- Talk with your baby and encourage your child to imitate your words.
- Say the sounds of animals, and encourage your child to imitate the sounds.
- Use flannel-board pictures, stuffed animals, or puppets to talk about the sounds of animals.
- Talk with your baby, and notice your child babbling back more and saying more sounds.
- Say nursery rhymes and do some actions with them.
- Sing to your baby. The more you sing with your baby, the more you will notice your baby trying to imitate you.
- Hold your baby and dance in rhythm to music you enjoy.
- Shake shakers in rhythm to music or a rhyme.
- Share board books with your baby, and talk about the pictures and the sounds of the animals.
- Even if you get tired of singing songs, saying animal sounds, saying nursery rhymes, and reading books over and over again, keep doing it because it helps your baby learn.
- Sing books with your child, and look for books of songs that you and your child enjoy.
- Visit the library with your baby.
- Talk with your toddler and encourage your child to imitate what you say.
- Say the sounds of animals, and encourage your toddler to repeat those sounds.
- Ask your toddler what sound an animal makes.
- Use flannel-board pictures, stuffed animals, or puppets to talk about the sounds of animals. Encourage your toddler to play with the props and try to say the sounds of the animals.
- Repeat a nursery rhyme and do some actions, and encourage your toddler to try to say the words and hear the rhythm and rhyme.
- Sing with your toddler, and encourage your child to sing some of the words, too.
- The more you sing with your toddler, the more your child is remembering and able to sing the song (even if you cannot understand the words).
- Sing and play rhythmic music, and encourage your toddler to move to the rhythm.
- When you sing songs or play music, use shakers or clap to emphasize the beat of the music.
- Read board books with your toddler, and talk about the pictures and the sounds of the animals.

- Even if you get tired of singing songs, saying animal sounds, saying nursery rhymes, and reading books over and over again, keep doing it because it helps your toddler learn.
- Sing books with your child, and look for books of songs that you and your child enjoy.
- Visit the library with your child.

You and Your Baby

☐ When I talk with my baby, my baby tries to imitate my words.

☐ When I say the sounds of animals, my baby listens.

☐ When I say the sounds of animals, my baby tries to imitate the sounds.

☐ I use flannel-board pictures, stuffed animals, or puppets to talk about the sounds of animals.

☐ The more I talk with my baby, the more I notice my baby babbling back and saying more sounds.

☐ When I say nursery rhymes and do some actions with them, my baby responds with interest.

☐ When I sing to my baby, my baby shows enjoyment.

☐ The more I sing with my baby, the more I notice my baby trying to imitate me.

☐ My baby enjoys it when I hold him or her and dance in rhythm to music I enjoy.

☐ When I shake the shaker in rhythm to music or a rhyme, my baby is alert to the sound.

☐ I share board books with my baby, talking about the pictures and the sounds of the animals.

☐ Even if I get tired of singing songs, saying animal sounds, saying nursery rhymes, and reading books over and over again, I still do it because it helps my baby learn.

☐ I visit the library with my baby.

You and Your Toddler

☐ When I talk with my toddler, my toddler tries to imitate what I say.

☐ When I say the sounds of animals, my toddler repeats those sounds.

☐ When I ask my toddler what sound an animal makes, my toddler answers with the sound of an animal (sometimes correctly).

☐ When I use the flannel-board pictures, stuffed animals, or puppets to talk about the sounds of animals, my toddler plays with the items and tries to say the sounds of the animals.

☐ The more I repeat a nursery rhyme and do some actions, the more my toddler tries to say the words and notice the rhythm and rhyme.

☐ When I sing with my toddler, my toddler sings some of the words, too.

☐ The more I sing with my toddler, the more my toddler is remembering and is able to sing the song (even if I cannot understand the words).

☐ When I sing with my toddler or play rhythmic music, my toddler moves to the rhythm.

☐ When we sing songs or play music, we use shakers or clap to emphasize the beat of the music.

☐ I read board books with my toddler, talking about the pictures and the sounds of the animals.

☐ Even if I get tired of singing songs, saying animal sounds, saying nursery rhymes, and reading books over and over again, I still do it because it helps my toddler learn.

Print Motivation

A child's interest in and enjoyment of books and reading

- When your baby chews or bites on a book, gently take it out of your child's mouth and talk about the pictures.
- Share books when your baby is not too tired and not too active but quietly alert.
- Choose books with bright colors and high contrast, which are more likely to keep your baby's attention.
- Read in a cheerful voice.
- Keep books handy. Store a few in the diaper bag, keep vinyl or cloth ones for bath time, have some near the changing table, and have some with your child's toys, so it is easy to share books anytime.
- When your baby gets fussy, continue reading another time.
- Even if you get tired of singing songs, saying nursery rhymes, and reading books over and over again, keep doing it because it helps your baby learn.
- Visit the library with your baby, and check out books to share.
- Make sure your baby sees you reading, too.
- Give your toddler choices when reading books together.
- Make sharing books with your toddler a special and enjoyable time.
- Keep your toddler engaged by encouraging your child to participate as you read the book.
- Keep books handy. Store some in the diaper bag, keep vinyl or cloth ones for bath time, have some near the changing table, and have some with your child's toys, so it is easy to share books anytime.
- When your toddler loses interest in the book, don't turn it into a power struggle. Pick up the book another time.
- Look for books on topics that your toddler is interested in.
- Even if you get tired of singing songs, saying animal sounds, saying nursery rhymes, and reading books over and over again, keep doing it because it helps your toddler learn.
- Make sure your toddler sees you reading. Tell your toddler when you read something interesting.
- Visit the library with your toddler, and check out books to share together.

You and Your Baby

- ☐ When my baby chews or bites on a book, I gently take it out of my baby's mouth and talk about the pictures.
- ☐ I share books when my baby is not too tired and not too active but quietly alert.
- ☐ I choose books with bright colors and high contrast, which are more likely to keep my baby's attention.
- ☐ I read in a cheerful voice.
- ☐ I keep books handy. I have some in the diaper bag, vinyl or cloth ones for bath time, some near the changing table, and a few with my child's toys, so it is easy to share books with my baby.

☐ When my baby gets fussy, I know I can continue reading another time.

☐ Even if I get tired of singing songs, saying nursery rhymes, and reading books over and over again, I still do it because it helps my baby learn.

☐ I visit the library with my baby and check out books to share.

☐ I make sure my baby sees me reading, too.

You and Your Toddler

☐ I give my toddler choices when reading books together.

☐ I try to make sharing books with my toddler a special and enjoyable time.

☐ I keep my toddler engaged by encouraging him or her to participate as we read the book.

☐ I keep books handy, storing some in the diaper bag, keeping vinyl or cloth ones for bath time, having some near the changing table, and having some with my child's toys, so it is easy to share books anytime.

☐ When my toddler loses interest in a book, I don't turn it into a power struggle. I can pick up the book another time.

☐ I look for books on topics that my toddler is interested in.

☐ Even if I get tired of singing songs, saying animal sounds, saying nursery rhymes, and reading books over and over again, I still do it because it helps my toddler learn.

☐ I make sure my toddler sees me reading. I tell my toddler when I read something interesting.

☐ I visit the library with my toddler and check out books to share together.

Print Awareness

Understanding that print has meaning, learning how to handle a book, understanding the direction of print, noticing print all around us

● When your baby bites or chews on books, this is how your baby is getting to know books and how they work. Gently take the book from your baby's mouth and talk about the pictures. Give your baby a rattle or something else to chew on.

● Encourage your baby to turn the pages in a book, even though your child may just bat at the pages.

● Point to pictures as you say the words.

● From time to time, point to the text on the pages of a book as you say the words.

● Because babies learn through their senses, when possible, show your baby the real item as you point out the picture in a book.

● When you are out walking, driving, or shopping, point out signs and tell your baby what they say.

● Visit the library with your baby, and check out books to share.

● Encourage your toddler to turn the pages in a book and help when needed.

● Point to pictures as you say the words.

● From time to time, point to the text on the pages of a book as you say the words. This helps your toddler understand that the written word represents what you are saying.

- Young children learn through their senses, so when possible, show your toddler the real item as you point out the picture in the book.
- When you read books with your toddler, point to the words in the title and in repeated phrases as you read them.
- When your toddler hands you a book upside down or backward, talk about starting the book at the front.
- When you are out walking, driving, or shopping, point out signs and tell your toddler what they say.
- Let your toddler see you writing a note, and then tell your child what it says.
- When you write a list, read it to your toddler, pointing to the words, and tell your child why you wrote the list.
- Encourage your toddler to draw and then talk about the picture.
- Encourage your toddler to scribble and talk about what it says.
- Visit the library with your toddler, and check out books to share together.

You and Your Baby

- ☐ When my baby bites or chews on books, I realize this is how my baby is getting to know books and how they work. I gently take the book from my baby's mouth and talk about the pictures. I give my baby a rattle or something else to chew on.
- ☐ I encourage my baby to turn the pages in a book, even though my baby's hands may just be batting at the pages.
- ☐ I point to pictures as I say the words.
- ☐ From time to time, I point to the text on the pages of a book as I say the words.
- ☐ Because babies learn through their senses, when possible, I show my baby the real item as I point out the picture in a book.
- ☐ When we are out walking, driving, or shopping, I point out signs and tell my baby what they say.
- ☐ I visit the library with my baby and check out books to share with my baby.

You and Your Toddler

- ☐ I encourage my toddler to turn the pages in a book and help when needed.
- ☐ I point to pictures as I say the words.
- ☐ From time to time, I point to the text or words on the pages of a book as I say the words. This helps my toddler understand that the written word represents what I am saying.
- ☐ Young children learn through their senses, so when possible, I show my toddler the real item as I point out the picture in the book.
- ☐ When I read books with my toddler, I point to the words in the title and in repeated phrases as I read them.
- ☐ When my toddler hands me a book upside down or backward, I talk about starting the book at the front.
- ☐ When we are out walking, driving, or shopping, I point out signs and tell my toddler what they say.
- ☐ I let my toddler see me writing a note and then tell my toddler what it says.

☐ When I write a list, I read it to my toddler, pointing to the words and telling my toddler why I wrote the list.

☐ I encourage my toddler to draw and then talk about the picture.

☐ I encourage my toddler to scribble and talk about what it says.

☐ I visit the library with my toddler and check out books to share together.

Vocabulary

Knowing the names of things, concepts, feelings, and ideas

● When you talk to your baby, use parentese: a higher pitch; short, simple sentences; and long vowel sounds.

● Use lots of different facial expressions with your baby, and notice that your baby will listen to you longer. Your baby learns more from you talking than from watching TV or DVDs.

● Even when you speak to your baby in parentese, use big words.

● Narrate your day to your baby, saying what you are doing as you do it or saying what your baby is doing.

● Say nursery rhymes and do some actions as you say them, because that is one way your baby learns new words.

● Share books with your baby, and talk about the pictures.

● When you read books with your baby, use big words, both the ones in the book and words you add.

● If you are reading a magazine, newspaper, or book, read some of it aloud to your baby.

● When you talk with your baby, notice how your child reacts with different expressions in his or her eyes and face.

● Even if you get tired of singing songs, saying nursery rhymes, and reading books over and over again, keep doing it because it helps your baby learn.

● Read books that have factual information because these books may have new words in them.

● Visit the library with your baby.

● Narrate your day to your toddler, saying what you are doing as you do it or saying what your child is doing.

● Try to find ways to encourage your toddler rather than just saying no. Offer choices, explain reasons, talk about feelings, and use words for self-control, such as *wait* or *gently*.

● The more you repeat a nursery rhyme and do some actions, the more your toddler may try to say the words.

● The more you sing with your toddler, the more your child is remembering and able to sing the song (even if you cannot understand all the words).

● Talk with your toddler and use words your child does not understand yet. Your toddler learns more from your talking than from watching TV or DVDs.

● When your toddler talks to you, repeat what your child says and then add some more words.

● Even if your toddler doesn't understand, explain what words mean or talk about what's going on around you.

● When you read books with your toddler, ask *what* questions and add more words.

- When you read books with your toddler, add words that your child doesn't know.
- Read some factual books with your toddler.
- Even if you get tired of singing songs, saying nursery rhymes, and reading books over and over again, keep doing it because it helps your toddler learn.

You and Your Baby

☐ When I talk to my baby, I use parentese.

☐ When I use lots of different facial expressions with my baby, I notice that my baby will listen to me longer. I know my baby learns more from my talking than from watching TV or DVDs.

☐ Even when I speak to my baby in parentese, I am using big words.

☐ I narrate my day to my baby, saying what I am doing as I do it or saying what my baby is doing.

☐ I say nursery rhymes and do some actions as I say them because that is one way my baby learns new words.

☐ I share books with my baby, talking about the pictures.

☐ When I read books with my baby, I use big words, both the ones in the book and words I add.

☐ If I am reading a magazine, newspaper, or book, I read some of it aloud to my baby.

☐ When I talk with my baby, I notice how my baby reacts with different expressions in his or her eyes and face.

☐ Even if I get tired of singing songs, saying nursery rhymes, and reading books over and over again, I still do it because it helps my baby learn.

☐ I visit the library with my baby.

You and Your Toddler

☐ I narrate my day to my toddler, saying what I am doing as I do it or saying what my child is doing.

☐ I try to find ways to encourage my toddler rather than just saying no. I offer choices, explain reasons, talk about feelings, and use words for self-control, such as *wait* or *gently*.

☐ The more I repeat a nursery rhyme and do some actions, the more my toddler tries to say the words.

☐ The more I sing with my toddler, the more my toddler is remembering and able to sing the song (even if I cannot understand all the words).

☐ As I talk with my toddler, I use words my toddler does not understand yet.

☐ I know my toddler learns more from my talking than from watching TV or DVDs.

☐ When my toddler talks to me, I repeat what my child says and then add some more words.

☐ Even if my toddler doesn't understand, that doesn't stop me—I explain what words mean or talk about what's going on around us.

☐ When I read books with my toddler, I ask *what* questions and add more words.

☐ When I read books with my toddler, I add words that my child doesn't know.

☐ I read some factual books with my toddler.

☐ Even if I get tired of singing songs, saying nursery rhymes, and reading books over and over again, I still do it because it helps my toddler learn.

Appendix A: Story-Time Planning Sheet

☐ Print motivation: Enjoyment of books

☐ Phonological awareness:

    ☐ Rhyming

    ☐ Rhythm

    ☐ Playing with silly or nonsense words

☐ Print awareness:

    ☐ With books

    ☐ In the environment

☐ Vocabulary:

    ☐ Introducing new words

    ☐ Explaining (not replacing) words

    ☐ Adding less-familiar words for description, action, feelings, concepts, and ideas

☐ Narrative skills:

    ☐ Encourage children to respond to simple questions

    ☐ Encourage children to repeat a word or phrase

    ☐ Ask questions about the story

    ☐ Use props, such as flannel story pieces or puppets

☐ Letter knowledge:

    ☐ Same and different

    ☐ Shapes

    ☐ Opposites

    ☐ Colors

☐ Practices:

    ☐ Read

    ☐ Write

    ☐ Sing

    ☐ Talk

    ☐ Play

Story-Time Activity	Early Literacy Connections and Notes	Materials Needed

Appendix B: Flannel Boards, Story Gloves, and Story Aprons

Throughout this book we have made suggestions to use flannel activities to enhance story times with children. There are different types of flannel activities and a variety of uses for flannel pieces. Flannel pieces also support all of the early literacy components. Story gloves and story aprons can be used in addition to or in place of using a flannel board.

The most important part of using flannels, gloves, and aprons with children is that you must be prepared. Practice the story, song, or rhyme. Have your pieces in order and ready to use. This will make the experience more fun and less stressful for you. Using props can help you remember the song or story because you see the next piece coming up.

Uses for Flannel Boards, Story Gloves, and Story Aprons

- **Interactive**—Flannel boards, gloves, and aprons are great tools to use to keep children's attention while telling a story or singing a song. If you have an active toddler, you can use flannel pieces to keep the child engaged. Allow toddlers to help put the pieces on the board or remove them from the board.
- **Songs and rhymes**—Use flannel pieces with songs and rhymes. They add visual, auditory, and tactile experiences.
- **Information**—Flannel pieces can be used to teach concepts such as colors, counting, and shapes.
- **Stories**—You can use flannels, gloves, and aprons to tell stories, or you can retell a story that the children are familiar with.

Supporting Early Literacy Components

- **Print Awareness**—When you are telling a story with flannels, place the pieces from left to right on the board. This reinforces the concept that we read from left to right in English. Also, as you tell a story or talk about the pictures you put on the board, children are beginning to make the connection that words can represent objects.
- **Phonological Awareness**—Songs and rhymes work well with flannel pieces. As children hear the sounds of words they are also incorporating tactile and visual learning.
- **Letter Knowledge**—Use flannel pieces to play with and talk about concepts such as shapes and colors. This helps build the foundation for learning about letters.
- **Vocabulary**—Make flannel pieces of objects that children are familiar with. You can then introduce new vocabulary related to those objects.

- **Background Knowledge**—Flannels are fun! They help keep children engaged, which will build excitement about reading. Flannels are a good way to tell a story. They help children learn about story structure.

There are a lot of options when considering what kind of flannel to use. You can purchase flannel boards, story gloves, "monkey mitts," story aprons. Commercially available boards come in a variety of sizes, from large to a small lap size, which is good for younger children. Commercially available flannel stories or pieces can be purchased from educational-supply sources. You can also make your own board or story glove and flannel pieces.

How to Make a Flannel Board

Materials
- Plywood, sturdy cardboard, or foam board
- Scissors, box cutter, or saw (adult use only)
- Felt
- Spray adhesive or glue
1. Cut the plywood, sturdy cardboard, or foam board to the desired size.
2. Spray the board with spray adhesive or spread glue on the board. (Note: Always use spray adhesive away from the children, in a well-ventilated area.)
3. Cover the board with felt.

How to Make a Story Glove

Materials
- Fabric gardening glove
- Velcro
- Glue or needle and thread
- Scissors
1. Cut the Velcro into fingertip-size pieces.
2. Glue or stitch a piece of Velcro onto each fingertip of the glove.

How to Make a Story Apron

Materials
- Fabric apron, smock, or oversized T-shirt
- Glue or needle and thread
- Velcro strips or felt
1. Cut strips of Velcro or a large piece of felt.
2. Sew or glue the Velcro or felt onto the front of the apron or shirt.
3. If there is room, glue or stitch patch pockets to hold your flannel pieces.

How to Make Pieces for Flannel Boards, Story Gloves, and Story Aprons

Materials

- Felt or nonfusible, heavyweight interfacing
- Old magazines or children's books
- Photographs
- Coloring books or resource books
- Clear contact paper or laminator
- Scissors
- Velcro
- Fabric fixative, such as Craft Bond
- Crayons or colored pencils
- Permanent marker
- Printer (optional)

1. To make your own flannel story pieces, be creative. Think about what you want to accomplish. Do you want to use pictures that you will label with the children, or do you want to tell a story?

2. You can make story pieces to use on flannel boards, story aprons, or story gloves from a variety of materials.

   - You can cut pictures from a magazine, cover them with contact paper, and put Velcro on the back.

   - You can recycle used books. If a book has been loved too much and the pages are falling out, save pictures that are still usable. Cover them with contact paper and put Velcro on the back.

   - You can use photographs. Add Velcro on the back, and use them on a flannel board.

3. To make fabric story pieces, use felt or nonfusible, heavyweight interfacing (available at fabric and craft stores).

4. Place the pattern from a coloring book, a resource book, or other source on top of the fabric.

5. Trace the pattern with a marker.

6. Color the pieces with markers, crayons, or colored pencils.

7. Cut out the finished pieces.

8. Spray the pieces with a fixative, such as Craft Bond. This will prevent the colors from rubbing off.

9. If you have an inkjet printer, you can cut the interfacing to letter size. Then, in a document, use clipart for the pictures in the song or story. Insert the interfacing into the paper feed and print the clipart on the interfacing. This is a good way to make multiple copies of figures so toddlers can play with flannel pieces, too.

Index

More Great Books From Gryphon House

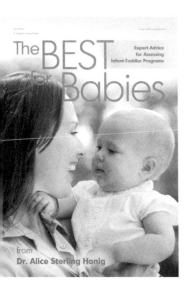

The Best for Babies
Expert Advice for Assessing Infant-Toddler Programs
Alice Sterling Honig, PhD

Caregiver-child interactions are critically important in promoting cognitive, language, and social-emotional learning in young children. This book offers an easy-to-use checklist to assess each teacher-child interpersonal relationship and the ways caregivers offer learning and living experiences for young children.

ISBN 978-0-87659-554-1, Item # 10704 | US $12.95 | PB, 7 x 10, 168 pp.

Encouraging Physical Activity in Infants
Steve Sanders, EdD

Babies are naturally active, and their movements help them explore their environment. Caregivers and parents can encourage their muscle development, strength, and balance with simple activities done with infants as young as six weeks old. From tummy time to crawling, scooting and standing, the first year of life lays the foundation for further development of gross motor skills as a toddler and preschooler.

ISBN: 978-0-87659-245-8, Item # 10057 | US $19.95 | PB, 6 x 9, 96 pp.

Encouraging Physical Activity in Toddlers
Steve Sanders, EdD

Toddlers are on the move almost constantly! Even though encouraging physical activity is not a problem, caregivers and parents can model new movements and skills and lay the foundation for them to enjoy physical activity as they grow. By helping toddlers understand how to develop physical skills, caregivers help them build confidence and have fun being active.

ISBN: 978-0-87659-050-8, Item # 10056 | US $19.95 | PB, 6 x 9, 144 pp.

More Great Books From Gryphon House

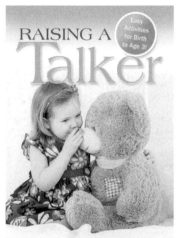

Raising a Talker
Easy Activities for Birth to Age 3!
Renate Zangl, PhD

Combining fun, easy-to-do activities with research based tips and developmental overviews, *Raising a Talker* helps parents and caregivers naturally transform play sessions into meaningful language-learning experiences. Little tweaks and easy changes in everyday play create nurturing environments where communication and discovery can flourish.

ISBN 978-0-87659-473-5, Item# 11505 | US $19.95 | PB, 8.5 x 11, 216 pp.

50 Fantastic Things to Do with Babies
Sally and Phill Featherstone

Parents and teachers can explore and experiment alongside young learners using these 50 simple activities that can be done easily with very little equipment. All of the ideas are suitable for newborns to around 20 months. Activities include baby massage, basic exploration, and hide-and-seek.

ISBN 978-0-87659-463-6, Item # 10046 | US $16.95 | PB, 6 x 99, 88 pp.

50 Fantastic Things to Do with Toddlers
Sally and Phill Featherstone

Using objects easily found in most homes, this collection of purposeful play experiences will help toddlers develop key skills. All of the ideas are suitable for toddlers from 16-36 months. Activities include making up rhyming words, simple pretend play, and much more.

ISBN 978-0-87659-465-0, Item # 10047 | US $16.95 | PB, 6 x 9, 88 pp.

More Great Books From Gryphon House

First Art for Toddlers & Twos
Open-Ended Art Experiences
MaryAnn F. Kohl with Renee Ramsey and Dana Bowman

More than 75 fun-filled art adventures will start children on a journey full of exploration and creativity! They will joyfully squeeze rainbows, make their own (safe) beads to string, and create their very own painted paper quilts.

ISBN 978-0-87659-399-8, Item # 10017 | US $19.95
PB, 11 x 8.5, 128 pp.

Many Languages, Building Connections
Supporting Infants and Toddlers Who Are Dual Language Learners
Karen N. Nemeth

This book provides everything caregivers need to create nurturing communities that support the linguistic and cultural development of children younger than the age of three.

ISBN 978-0-87659-389-9, Item # 10004 | US $16.95 | PB, 8 .5 x 11, 128 pp.

Story S-t-r-e-t-c-h-e-r-s for Infants, Toddlers, and Twos
Shirley C. Raines, Karen Miller, and Leah Curry-Rood

It's never too early to read to a child, especially when you have *Story S-t-r-e-t-c-h-e-r-s!* The youngest children love the repetition of words and experiences that stories provide. *Story S-t-r-e-t-c-h-e-r-s* contains 80 age-appropriate children's books and 240 ways to s-t-r-e-t-c-h the stories in new ways to enhance the learning process.

ISBN 978-0-87659-274-8, Item # 18931 | US $19.95 | PB, 8.5 x 11, 192 pp.

More Great Books From Gryphon House

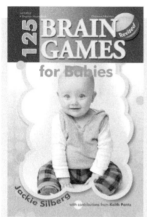

125 Brain Games for Babies
Revised Edition
Jackie Silberg

Filled with everyday opportunities to contribute to the brain development of children from birth through 12 months, these simple games create the brain connections needed for future learning.

ISBN 978-0-87659-391-2, Item # 13533 | US $16.95 | PB, 6 x 9, 144 pp.

125 Brain Game for Toddlers
Revised Edition
Jackie Silberg

A fun-filled collection of ways to lay the groundwork for future learning! Each game is accompanied by information on related brain research and a description of how the activity promotes brain power in children.

ISBN 978-0-87659-392-9, Item # 13534 | US $16.95 | PB, 6 x 9, 144 pp.

The Complete Learning Spaces Book for Infants and Toddlers
Rebecca Isbell and Christy Isbell

This book includes ideas for planning, creating, using, and evaluating learning spaces that captivate infants and toddlers and encourage the developmental process.

ISBN 978-0-87659-293-9, Item # 16917 | US $29.95 | PB, 5 x 11, 352 pp.

Teaching Infants, Toddlers, and Twos with Special Needs
Clarissa Willis, PhD

Written to address the needs of children with developmental delays, as well as those children at risk for developing special needs. This book is for all teachers and directors who work with infants, toddlers, and twos, including both special educators and educators working with typically developing children.

ISBN 978-0-87659-069-0, Item # 15089 | US $19.95 | PB, 8.5 x 11, 160 pp.